HOW TO MAKE
Picture
Frames

American Woodworker

HOW TO MAKE
Picture
Frames

12 SIMPLE TO STYLISH PROJECTS
from the Experts at American Woodworker

FOX CHAPEL
PUBLISHING

Published by Fox Chapel Publishing Company, Inc., 1970 Broad St., East Petersburg, PA 17520, 717-560-4703, *www.FoxChapelPublishing.com*

American Woodworker, ISSN 1074-9152, USPS 738-710, is published bimonthly by Woodworking Media, LLC, 90 Sherman St., Cambridge, MA 02140, *www.AmericanWoodworker.com*.

Library of Congress Control Number: 2009053477
ISBN-13: 978-1-56523-459-8
ISBN-10: 1-56523-459-6

Library of Congress Cataloging-in-Publication Data

How to make picture frames.

   p. cm.

Includes index.

ISBN 978-1-56523-459-8

1. Picture frames and framing. I. Fox Chapel Publishing.

TT899.2.H693 2010

749'.7--dc22

2009053477

To learn more about the other great books from Fox Chapel Publishing, or to find a retailer near you, call toll-free 800-457-9112 or visit us at *www.FoxChapelPublishing.com*.

Note to Authors: We are always looking for talented authors to write new books in our area of woodworking, design, and related crafts. Please send a brief letter describing your idea to Acquisition Editor, 1970 Broad Street, East Petersburg, PA 17520.

Printed in China
Third printing

Contents

Featured Projects

BASIC PICTURE FRAMES

Rustic Picture Frame, page 60

Photo Album, page 72

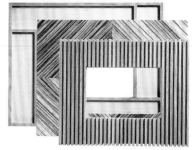

Three One-Day Picture Frames, page 74

MAKING MULTIPLE FRAMES

Router Moldings, page 40

**Three Router-Made
Picture Frames,** page 46

ANTIQUE AND CONTEMPORARY FRAMES

Oval Picture Frames, page 62

Craftsman Frame, page 84

Fab Frames, page 92

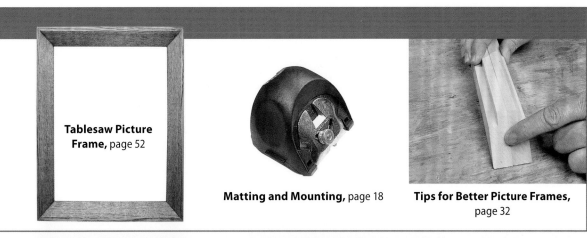

Picture Frame Techniques

Few things are as personally rewarding as displaying family treasures with beautiful frames you make yourself. Here's your chance to learn how to make your own frames for family or travel photos, children's art, samplers, paintings—anything you want to hang on the wall, display on a shelf, or preserve in an album. A variety of styles and woods helps you choose the perfect frame for each photo, piece of artwork, or other image you wish to display.

From relatively simple frames to more complex and highly decorated ones, you will find clear instructions with a wealth of illustrations. Step-by-step photos clearly show the sequence of tasks. Technical illustrations also provide essential information.

Use "Featured Projects" on page 6 to help you choose your projects. You will find ways to make multiple frames, as well as an interesting choice of frame styles. Some have a vintage look. Others have a contemporary or even whimsical style. Instructions for making two distinctive hall mirrors complete the collection.

How to Make Picture Frames is a collection of some of the best projects published by *American Woodworker* magazine. *American Woodworker* magazine is committed to providing woodworkers with the most accurate and up-to-date plans and information—including new ideas, product and tool reviews, workshop tips, and more.

by TIM JOHNSON

Weekend Picture Frames

CREATE EXTRAORDINARY FRAMES WITH ORDINARY ROUTER BITS

Here's a fun way to save money, be creative, make something useful, and use up scrap stock: make your own picture frames. You can start from scratch and have finished frames in a day or less, and the only tools you need are a tablesaw and a router table. The challenge is to create unique profiles using the router bits you already have.

The frames and instructions that follow will get you started. You probably don't have all the same bits, but that doesn't matter. Just substitute and experiment. You'll find that a little tinkering yields an amazing range of profiles.

Most frames are made using small stock, so be sure to work safely. Always use guards, featherboards and push sticks. Never use stock less than 12" long. Create profiles on long stock; then cut individual frame pieces from the profiled stock. Similarly, use wide stock to create thin pieces; rout the profile, then cut to final thickness. Rout large or deep profiles in multiple passes, raising the bit or moving the fence in small increments before each pass.

Create unique frames by experimenting. All of the frames shown here were made by combining tablesaw cuts and profiles made with these common router bits.

½" Cove

½" Roundover

¼" Roundover

⅜" Rabbet

¾" Round Nose

⅜" Roundover

¼" Half-Round

45° Chamfer

¼" Straight

⅛" Roundover

½" Straight

½" Round Nose

⅛" Round Nose

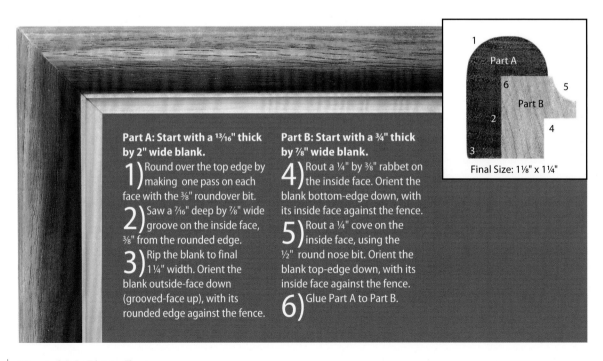

Part A: Start with a ¹³⁄₁₆" thick by 2" wide blank.

1) Round over the top edge by making one pass on each face with the ⅜" roundover bit.

2) Saw a ⁷⁄₁₆" deep by ⅞" wide groove on the inside face, ⅜" from the rounded edge.

3) Rip the blank to final 1¼" width. Orient the blank outside-face down (grooved-face up), with its rounded edge against the fence.

Part B: Start with a ¾" thick by ⅞" wide blank.

4) Rout a ¼" by ⅜" rabbet on the inside face. Orient the blank bottom-edge down, with its inside face against the fence.

5) Rout a ¼" cove on the inside face, using the ½" round nose bit. Orient the blank top-edge down, with its inside face against the fence.

6) Glue Part A to Part B.

Part A

Part B

1

6

5

2

4

3

Final Size: 1⅛" x 1¼"

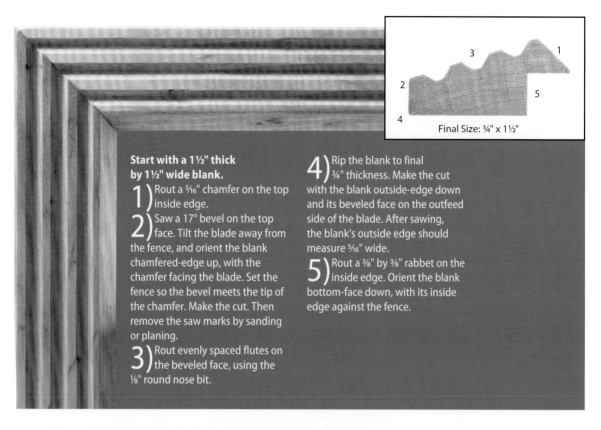

Final Size: ¾" x 1½"

Start with a 1½" thick by 1½" wide blank.

1) Rout a ⁵⁄₁₆" chamfer on the top inside edge.

2) Saw a 17° bevel on the top face. Tilt the blade away from the fence, and orient the blank chamfered-edge up, with the chamfer facing the blade. Set the fence so the bevel meets the tip of the chamfer. Make the cut. Then remove the saw marks by sanding or planing.

3) Rout evenly spaced flutes on the beveled face, using the ⅛" round nose bit.

4) Rip the blank to final ¾" thickness. Make the cut with the blank outside-edge down and its beveled face on the outfeed side of the blade. After sawing, the blank's outside edge should measure ⁵⁄₁₆" wide.

5) Rout a ⅜" by ⅜" rabbet on the inside edge. Orient the blank bottom-face down, with its inside edge against the fence.

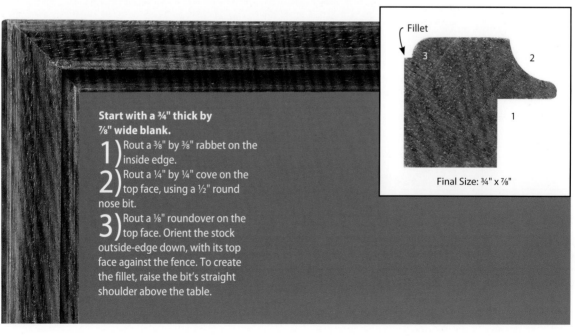

Fillet

Final Size: ¾" x ⅞"

Start with a ¾" thick by ⅞" wide blank.

1) Rout a ⅜" by ⅜" rabbet on the inside edge.

2) Rout a ¼" by ¼" cove on the top face, using a ½" round nose bit.

3) Rout a ⅛" roundover on the top face. Orient the stock outside-edge down, with its top face against the fence. To create the fillet, raise the bit's straight shoulder above the table.

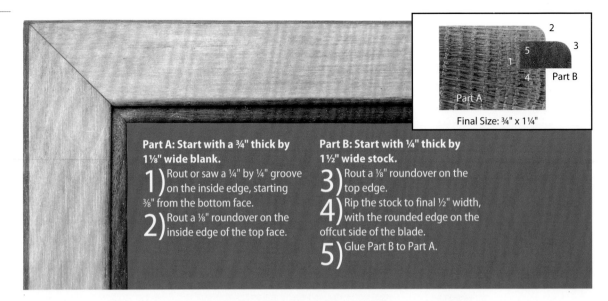

Final Size: ¾" x 1¼"

Part A: Start with a ¾" thick by 1⅛" wide blank.

1) Rout or saw a ¼" by ¼" groove on the inside edge, starting ⅜" from the bottom face.

2) Rout a ⅛" roundover on the inside edge of the top face.

Part B: Start with ¼" thick by 1½" wide stock.

3) Rout a ⅛" roundover on the top edge.

4) Rip the stock to final ½" width, with the rounded edge on the offcut side of the blade.

5) Glue Part B to Part A.

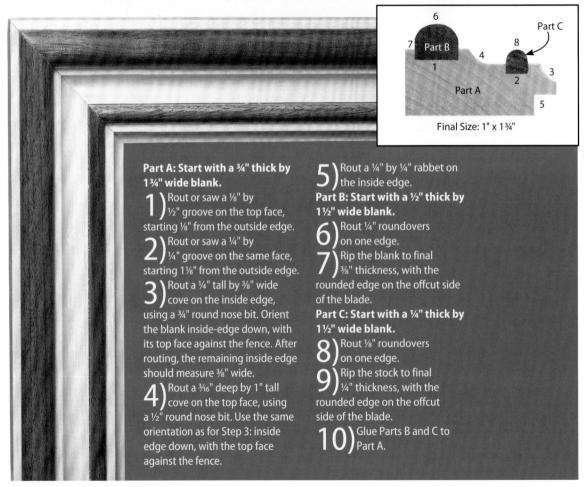

Final Size: 1" x 1¾"

Part A: Start with a ¾" thick by 1¾" wide blank.

1) Rout or saw a ⅛" by ½" groove on the top face, starting ⅛" from the outside edge.

2) Rout or saw a ¼" by ¼" groove on the same face, starting 1⅛" from the outside edge.

3) Rout a ¼" tall by ⅜" wide cove on the inside edge, using a ¾" round nose bit. Orient the blank inside-edge down, with its top face against the fence. After routing, the remaining inside edge should measure ⅜" wide.

4) Rout a 3⁄16" deep by 1" tall cove on the top face, using a ½" round nose bit. Use the same orientation as for Step 3: inside edge down, with the top face against the fence.

5) Rout a ¼" by ¼" rabbet on the inside edge.

Part B: Start with a ½" thick by 1½" wide blank.

6) Rout ¼" roundovers on one edge.

7) Rip the blank to final ⅜" thickness, with the rounded edge on the offcut side of the blade.

Part C: Start with a ¼" thick by 1½" wide blank.

8) Rout ⅛" roundovers on one edge.

9) Rip the stock to final ¼" thickness, with the rounded edge on the offcut side of the blade.

10) Glue Parts B and C to Part A.

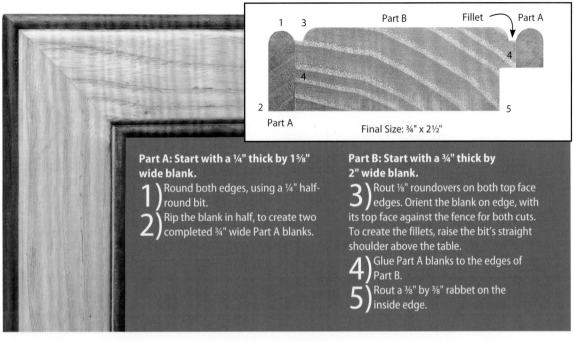

1 3   Part B   Fillet   Part A

4

2

Part A

5

Final Size: ¾" x 2½"

Part A: Start with a ¼" thick by 1⅝" wide blank.

1) Round both edges, using a ¼" half-round bit.

2) Rip the blank in half, to create two completed ¾" wide Part A blanks.

Part B: Start with a ¾" thick by 2" wide blank.

3) Rout ⅛" roundovers on both top face edges. Orient the blank on edge, with its top face against the fence for both cuts. To create the fillets, raise the bit's straight shoulder above the table.

4) Glue Part A blanks to the edges of Part B.

5) Rout a ⅜" by ⅜" rabbet on the inside edge.

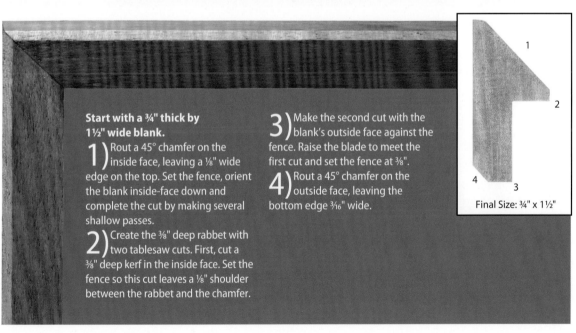

1

2

4

3

Final Size: ¾" x 1½"

Start with a ¾" thick by 1½" wide blank.

1) Rout a 45° chamfer on the inside face, leaving a ⅛" wide edge on the top. Set the fence, orient the blank inside-face down and complete the cut by making several shallow passes.

2) Create the ⅜" deep rabbet with two tablesaw cuts. First, cut a ⅜" deep kerf in the inside face. Set the fence so this cut leaves a ⅛" shoulder between the rabbet and the chamfer.

3) Make the second cut with the blank's outside face against the fence. Raise the blade to meet the first cut and set the fence at ⅜".

4) Rout a 45° chamfer on the outside face, leaving the bottom edge ³⁄₁₆" wide.

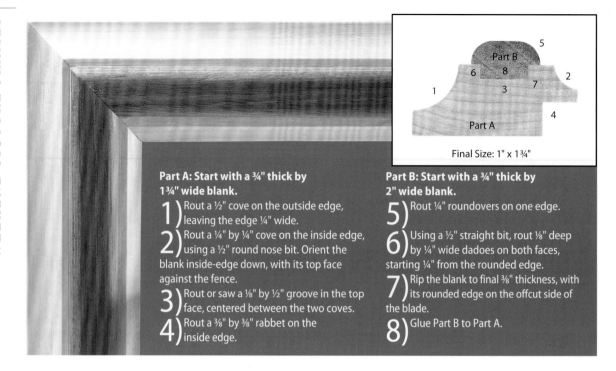

Final Size: 1" x 1¾"

Part A: Start with a ¾" thick by 1¾" wide blank.

1) Rout a ½" cove on the outside edge, leaving the edge ¼" wide.

2) Rout a ¼" by ¼" cove on the inside edge, using a ½" round nose bit. Orient the blank inside-edge down, with its top face against the fence.

3) Rout or saw a ⅛" by ½" groove in the top face, centered between the two coves.

4) Rout a ⅜" by ⅜" rabbet on the inside edge.

Part B: Start with a ¾" thick by 2" wide blank.

5) Rout ¼" roundovers on one edge.

6) Using a ½" straight bit, rout ⅛" deep by ¼" wide dadoes on both faces, starting ¼" from the rounded edge.

7) Rip the blank to final ⅜" thickness, with its rounded edge on the offcut side of the blade.

8) Glue Part B to Part A.

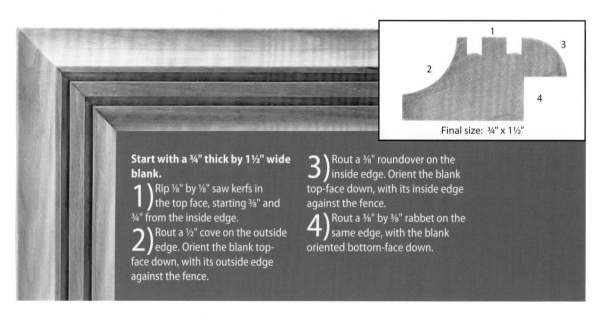

Final size: ¾" x 1½"

Start with a ¾" thick by 1½" wide blank.

1) Rip ⅛" by ⅛" saw kerfs in the top face, starting ⅜" and ¾" from the inside edge.

2) Rout a ½" cove on the outside edge. Orient the blank top-face down, with its outside edge against the fence.

3) Rout a ⅜" roundover on the inside edge. Orient the blank top-face down, with its inside edge against the fence.

4) Rout a ⅜" by ⅜" rabbet on the same edge, with the blank oriented bottom-face down.

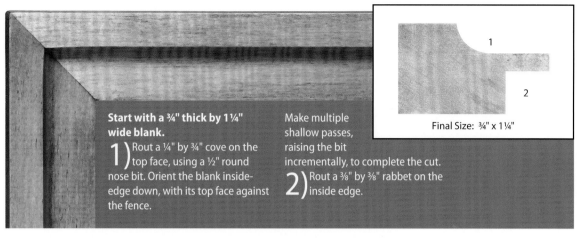

Start with a ¾" thick by 1¼" wide blank.

1) Rout a ¼" by ¾" cove on the top face, using a ½" round nose bit. Orient the blank inside-edge down, with its top face against the fence.

Make multiple shallow passes, raising the bit incrementally, to complete the cut.

2) Rout a ⅜" by ⅜" rabbet on the inside edge.

Final Size: ¾" x 1¼"

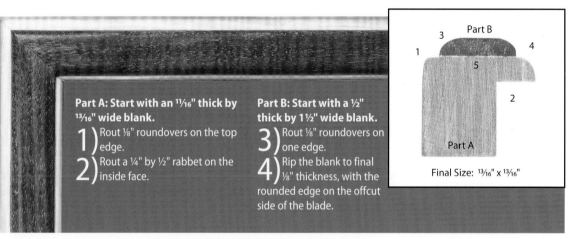

Part A: Start with an ¹¹⁄₁₆" thick by ¹³⁄₁₆" wide blank.

1) Rout ⅛" roundovers on the top edge.

2) Rout a ¼" by ½" rabbet on the inside face.

Part B: Start with a ½" thick by 1½" wide blank.

3) Rout ⅛" roundovers on one edge.

4) Rip the blank to final ⅛" thickness, with the rounded edge on the offcut side of the blade.

Part B

Part A

Final Size: ¹³⁄₁₆" x ¹³⁄₁₆"

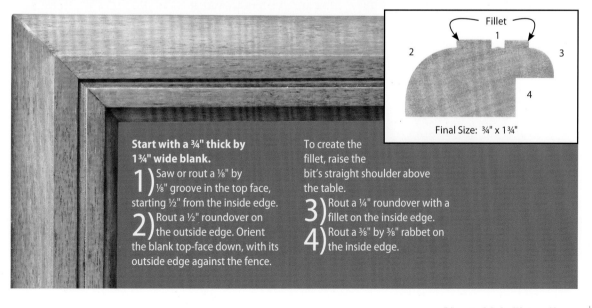

Start with a ¾" thick by 1¾" wide blank.

1) Saw or rout a ⅛" by ⅛" groove in the top face, starting ½" from the inside edge.

2) Rout a ½" roundover on the outside edge. Orient the blank top-face down, with its outside edge against the fence.

To create the fillet, raise the bit's straight shoulder above the table.

3) Rout a ¼" roundover with a fillet on the inside edge.

4) Rout a ⅜" by ⅜" rabbet on the inside edge.

Fillet

Final Size: ¾" x 1¾"

Matting and Mounting

IMPROVING AESTHETICS AND PROTECTING YOUR ART

Matting

Most artwork looks better when a border of mat board separates the frame from the picture. Beyond its aesthetic value, the mat also separates the artwork from the glass where condensation can cause damage. Here's a simple step-by-step procedure for cutting the mat opening and mounting the artwork using simple shop-made jigs and tools.

The first step, and probably the one that's most intimidating, is choosing the color and size of the border. A few rules of thumb should clear things up:

- Choose a mat color that reflects a dominant color in the art.

- Stay away from bold colors that might distract the eye from the art. Off-white is usually a safe choice.

- The border created by the mat opening should be wider than the frame. Two- to 3-in. borders are good for most common sizes.

- Make the bottom border 10 percent wider to visually anchor the artwork in the frame.

- When in doubt, visit a framing store and look at some examples of similar-size artwork for inspiration.

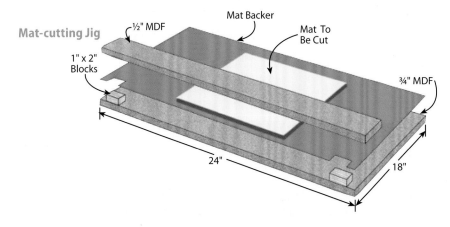

Mat-cutting Jig

½" MDF

Mat Backer

Mat To Be Cut

1" x 2" Blocks

¾" MDF

24"

18"

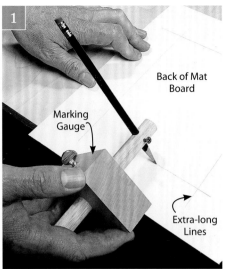

Lay out the mat opening with a marking gauge. You can easily make your own from a block of wood and some ⅝-in. dowel.

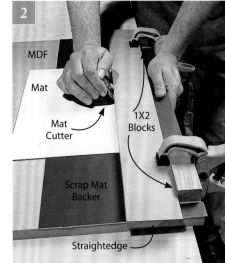

Use a mat-cutting jig to cut the opening. This straightforward jig prevents the straightedge from being pushed aside by the cutter while holding the mat secure. The jig is nothing more than a piece of MDF with a couple of 1x2 blocks glued to one edge. A piece of scrap mat board is used as a backer for the knife to cut into.

Mat Cutter

Oops!

Oh, no. Can you believe it? I didn't cut all the way into the corners of the mat opening. Next time I'll get that cutter recommended in Photo 2. It has index marks to show you exactly where to stop the cut for perfect corners. In the meantime, I carefully slipped a fresh utility razor into the 45-degree slit from the top side of the mat. Then I rocked the blade gently into the corner to finish the cut. Whew! That mat board is too pricey to waste.

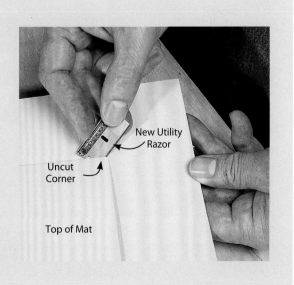

How to mount Artwork

Here's how to expertly mount photos and artwork to protect them from moisture and damage.

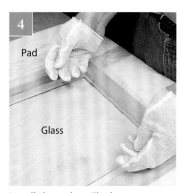

1 Mat Opening · Tape Hinge · Mounting Board

Hinge the mat to a mounting board (a solid piece of acid-free matte or foam core board). Butt the top edges together and secure them with acid-free mounting tape.

2 Artwork

Position the artwork in the mat's opening. Keep the artwork from shifting by weighing it down with a block of wood that has acid-free matte board glued to its bottom.

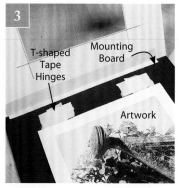

3 T-shaped Tape Hinges · Mounting Board · Artwork

Mount the art to the mounting board using T-shaped hinges, which allow the artwork to expand and contract, staying wrinkle-free. Fasten the tape sticky-side up on the back side of the artwork, at the top corners only. Place a second piece of tape, sticky-side down, as close to the artwork as possible.

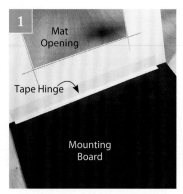

4 Pad · Glass

Install clean glass. The best way to keep fingerprints, dirt, and lint off the matte and glass is to wear darkroom gloves. Install the artwork, mounting board, and mat.

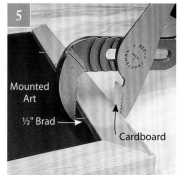

5 Mounted Art · ½" Brad · Cardboard

Secure the assembly with brads or glazier's points. The safest way to push in the brads is by using a pair of adjustable pliers.

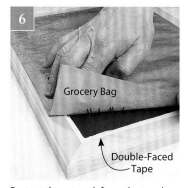

6 Grocery Bag · Double-Faced Tape

Protect the artwork from dust and insects by sealing the back of the frame with a paper dust shield. A grocery bag or kraft paper works fine. After installing the paper, dampen it with a sponge. The paper will shrink as it dries, leaving a tight, wrinkle-free dust shield.

Mounting

Hinge the mat to the mounting board to keep the opening in the mat aligned properly with the artwork (Photo 3). Once the artwork is positioned in the mat opening (Photo 4), it is secured to the mounting board with two T-hinges (Photo 5). The hinges allow the artwork to hang freely on the mounting board, which prevents the artwork from buckling with changes in humidity.

Tip

Use acid-free tape for the hinges. It's reversible and won't contribute to the deterioration of the artwork.

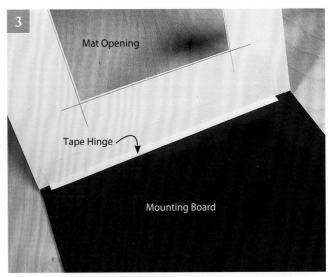

Hinge the mat to the mounting board. Simply butt the top edges together with the mat board face down and the mounting board face-up, and secure with acid-free mounting tape.

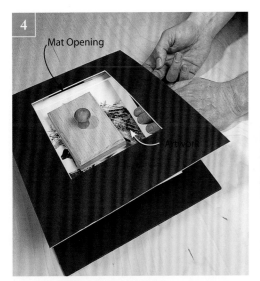

Position the artwork in the mat opening. A simple block of wood with some acid-free mat board glued on the bottom keeps the artwork from shifting as the mat is raised and lowered for positioning. Don't be tempted to use your finger as a hold-down. Acids and oils from your skin will cause the artwork to deteriorate over time.

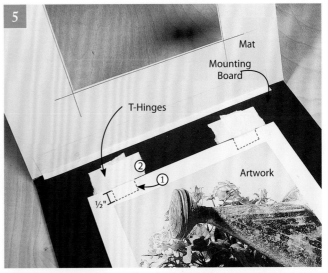

Mount the art to the mounting board with T-hinges.
1. Fasten tape sticky-side-up on the backside of the artwork, at the top corners only.
2. A second piece of tape is placed sticky-side-down across the first, as close to the artwork as possible. With this technique, the artwork is free to expand and contract.

by RANDY JOHNSON

Photo Frames by the Dozen

TWO JIGS LET YOU CRANK THEM OUT FLAWLESSLY!

Everyone I know has a drawer stuffed with photos that are waiting to be framed. What often keeps us from getting those treasures up on the wall is the high cost of professional framing.

If you've ever tried making picture frames, I'll bet you got frustrated cutting the miters and clamping the corners. We've got the perfect solution.

We've designed a great looking two-part frame that's downright cheap and easy to make. The pieces are small, so you can use up some of that scrap wood you've been unable to part with. Plus, with our surefire mitering and clamping jigs, you can make frames by the dozen.

The frame and jigs shown here are set up for 8 x 10 or smaller photos. By using different mats, you can use one frame size for different-size photos. You can also make the frame and jigs larger or smaller to custom-fit almost any size picture.

Our frame design is perfect for holiday gift making because it fits a variety of photos.

8 x 10 photo mounted without a mat in a cherry and walnut frame.

Two small photos mounted with a twin mat in a walnut frame.

4 x 6 photo mounted with a double mat in a mahogany and walnut frame.

5 x 7 photo mounted with a vertical mat in a maple and walnut frame.

Our frame design has two parts, which can be made of different woods or even used as two *separate* frames!

Tools and Materials

To make the frames you will need a tablesaw, a router and router table, plus a dado blade and router bits. To build the jigs you will also need a hand drill, jigsaw, hacksaw and a few spring clamps.

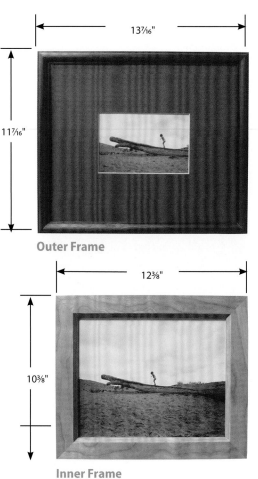

Outer Frame

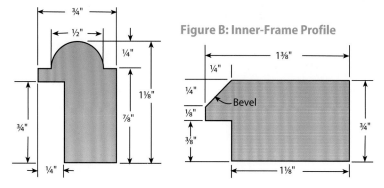

Inner Frame

Figure A: Outer-Frame Profile

Figure B: Inner-Frame Profile

Machining the Frame Material

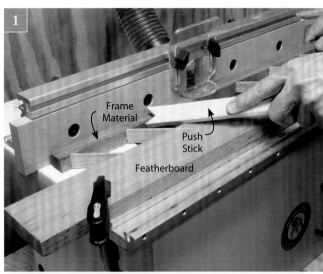

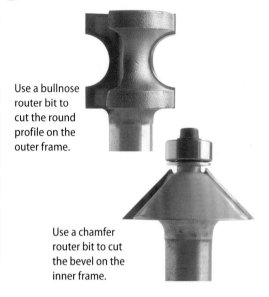

Use a bullnose router bit to cut the round profile on the outer frame.

Use a chamfer router bit to cut the bevel on the inner frame.

Rout the frame profiles on your router table. Keep things safe by using featherboards and push sticks.

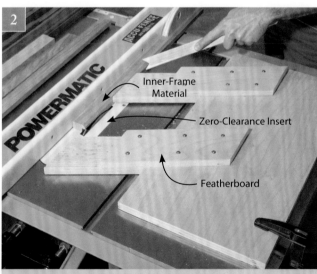

Caution! Blade guard must be removed for this cut.

Cut the rabbet in the inner-frame material with a dado blade. Use a zero-clearance insert to fully support the frame material and featherboards to keep the material against the fence while making the rabbet.

Caution! Blade guard must be removed for this cut.

Cut the rabbet in the outer-frame material. Adjust the outfeed featherboard so it rides inside the rabbet.

Making and Using the Miter Sled

This tablesaw sled makes perfect miters every time. You'll be able to quickly cut accurate multiple frame parts. Start by cutting all the parts for the sled (Fig. C and Detail 1). You'll have to size the guide rails to fit your tablesaw because slot sizes vary between saw brands. Make the guide rails so they slide freely, yet have minimal side-to-side movement. Make them about ¹⁄₁₆-in. thinner than the depth of the slots in your tablesaw. Also make a pair of ⅛-in.-thick spacer strips to use when gluing the guide rails to the sled board (Photo 4).

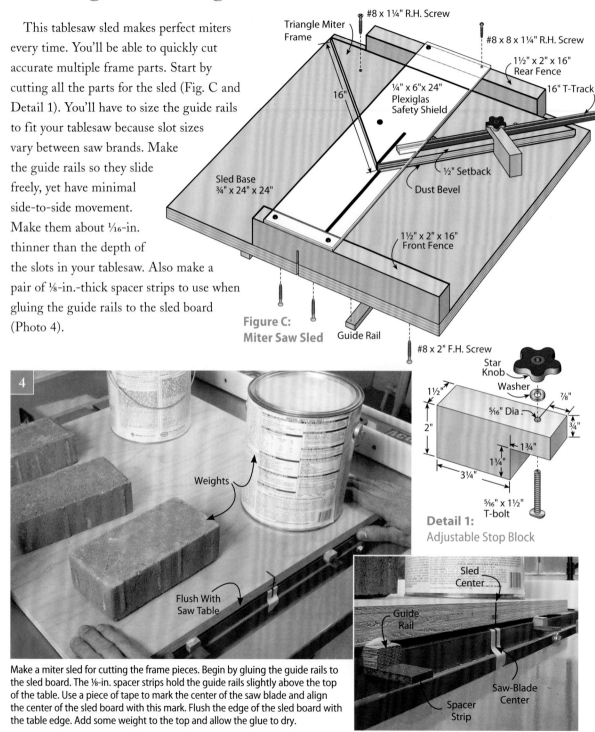

Triangle Miter Frame

#8 x 1¼" R.H. Screw

#8 x 8 x 1¼" R.H. Screw

1½" x 2" x 16" Rear Fence

16" T-Track

16"

¼" x 6"x 24" Plexiglas Safety Shield

½" Setback

Sled Base ¾" x 24" x 24"

Dust Bevel

1½" x 2" x 16" Front Fence

Figure C: Miter Saw Sled

Guide Rail

#8 x 2" F.H. Screw

Star Knob

Washer

1½"

⁵⁄₁₆" Dia.

⅞"

¾"

2"

5⁄₁₆" Dia

1¾"

1¼"

3¼"

5⁄₁₆" x 1½" T-bolt

Detail 1: Adjustable Stop Block

Weights

Flush With Saw Table

Sled Center

Guide Rail

Saw-Blade Center

Spacer Strip

Make a miter sled for cutting the frame pieces. Begin by gluing the guide rails to the sled board. The ⅛-in. spacer strips hold the guide rails slightly above the top of the table. Use a piece of tape to mark the center of the saw blade and align the center of the sled board with this mark. Flush the edge of the sled board with the table edge. Add some weight to the top and allow the glue to dry.

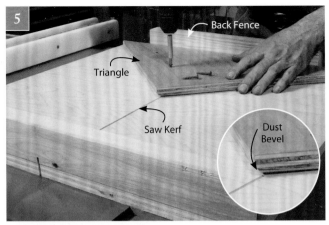

Center the tip of the plywood triangle with the middle of the saw kerf and against the rear sled fence. The dust bevel on the bottom edge prevents dust buildup.

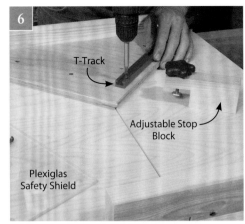

Screw the T-track and the safety shield in place. Add the stop block and the sled is ready to use.

First cut. Cut the first miter with the frame material on the right side of the miter sled. We marked our miter sled to remind us of the cutting order.

Second cut. Cut the second miter with the frame material on the left side of the miter sled. Set the adjustable stop block for the required lengths.

After attaching the guide rails, add the front and rear fences. Put the sled on your tablesaw with the blade raised about 1 in. Now slide the saw sled into the blade until the plywood is cut to about half of its width.

Next, make the plywood triangle. Start with a 16-in.-square piece of plywood and cut it diagonally with a jigsaw. Don't forget to rout the dust bevel on the bottom side of the triangle. This bevel helps prevent sawdust from building up against the triangle and causing miter-fitting problems (see Oops!, page 29).

Center the triangle on the saw kerf and attach it to the sled base with screws (Photo 5). Complete the saw sled with the addition of the T-track, adjustable stop block and the safety shield (Photo 6).

Cutting frame parts with this miter sled is a simple two-step process (Photos 7 and 8).

Making and Using the Clamping Jig

This clamping jig takes the pain out of gluing and clamping miters. Unlike the old one-corner-at-a-time clamps, ours takes care of all four corners at once!

The clamping jig shown here is made specifically to fit our frame sizes. You can clamp other size frames by making the clamping jig larger or smaller.

To make the jig, cut the parts according to Fig. D. Drill ¾-in. holes, then cut out the glue drip slots with a jigsaw. Next, drill for the threaded inserts and screw them in place. Now glue the sides to the base. To ensure perfectly square frames, the jig sides that don't have threaded inserts must be perfectly square to each other (Photo 9).

To complete your clamping jig, make the filler boards (Fig. E). These boards keep the frame centered in the jig, help distribute the clamping pressure evenly, and protect the frame from the ends of the clamping bolts.

Make a clamping jig to help assemble the frames. Glue and clamp the sides to the jig base. Make sure the insides of the sides without threaded inserts are perfectly square to each other.

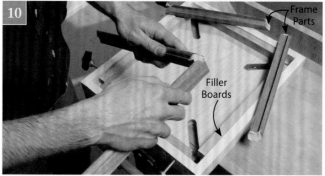

Rub glue on the end grain of your frame parts. Let it dry about 10 or 15 seconds. If it seems to soak in a lot, add a little more glue, rub again and let the parts rest for another 5 or 10 seconds. When the glue seems a bit tacky (no longer runny), you can put the parts in the clamping jig. Note that the filler boards are already in place.

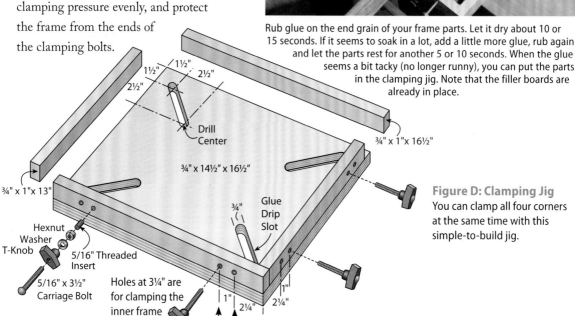

Figure D: Clamping Jig
You can clamp all four corners at the same time with this simple-to-build jig.

Drill Center

¾" x 14½" x 16½"

¾" x 1" x 16½"

¾" x 1" x 13"

Glue Drip Slot

Hexnut
Washer
T-Knob

5/16" Threaded Insert

5/16" x 3½" Carriage Bolt

Holes at 3¼" are for clamping the inner frame

Holes at 2¼" are for clamping the outer frame

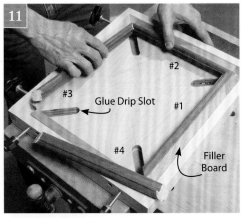

11

12

Assemble the frame in the clamping jig one part at a time. Start with the long side, part 1, and add parts 2, 3 and 4 in order. Line up the miters and you're ready to apply clamping pressure.

Follow the steps in Photos 11 and 12 to clamp up your frames. If clamping one frame at a time seems too slow for you, make several clamping jigs and you'll really be in the production business.

Apply clamping pressure a little bit at a time. Turn each clamp lightly at first. Double-check that the miters are still lined up and then apply more pressure. When the risk of slippage seems to be gone, apply firm pressure to the clamping bolts. Don't overtighten. These are small joints and don't require a ton of clamping pressure to bring them together. It may take you a couple of frames to get the hang of clamping all four corners at the same time, but once you do you'll be amazed at how fast you can make perfect frames. After the glue dries, sand the frames. The inner and outer frames can be glued together before finishing or brad-nailed together after finishing.

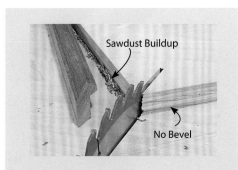

Oops!

Sawdust buildup can keep your frame material from lying tightly against the triangle fence. This causes miter-alignment problems later on. We learned this the hard way when we built our prototype miter sled (photo, above). That's why it's important to bevel the bottom of the triangle fence to give the sawdust a place to go.

Figure E : Clamping Jig Filler Boards
Make two of each size.

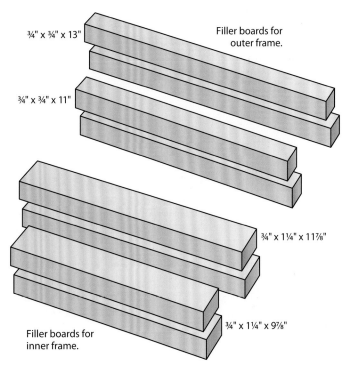

Finish the Frames

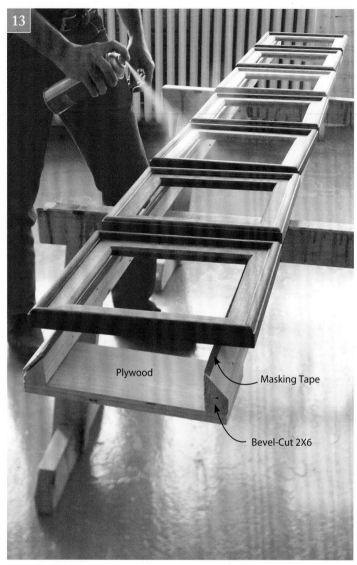

13

Plywood

Masking Tape

Bevel-Cut 2X6

Have some fun! Try using different woods and different finishes.

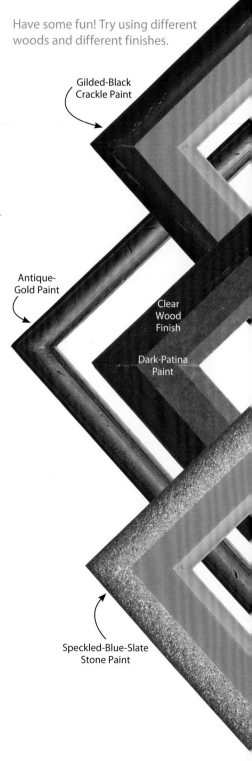

Gilded-Black Crackle Paint

Antique-Gold Paint

Clear Wood Finish

Dark-Patina Paint

Speckled-Blue-Slate Stone Paint

Finish your frames. A spray-on finish is the easiest. We bevel-cut a 2x6 in half and screwed on a piece of plywood at both ends to make a simple finishing rack. The open design allows the overspray to blow through rather than bounce back onto the frames. Replace the masking tape when it gets covered with finish.

FENDER WASHERS FOR MOUNTING PICTURES

by LARRY JENKINS

I enjoy making picture frames but always found it a pain to use tacks or staples to hold the picture in place. Plus, tacks and staples are hard to remove when you want to change the picture. That's why I developed this method for holding the picture, glass, matting, and backing board in the frame. I use 1-in.-diameter fender washers and #6 by ⅜-in. pan-head screws. I drill the recess for the washer with a Forstner bit and make the recess deep enough so the washer will bear against the backing board to hold everything snug.

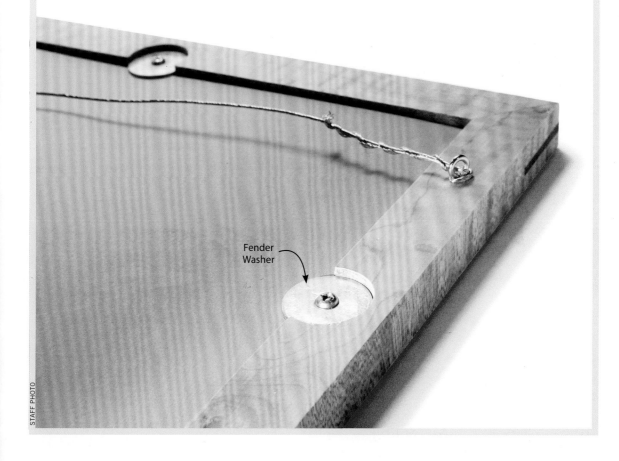

Fender Washer

STAFF PHOTO

by DAVE MUNKITTRICK

Tips for Better Picture Frames

FRAME LIKE A PRO WITH SIMPLE TOOLS

Easy Brad Pusher

One-half-inch brads are ideal for securing mounted artwork and glass in a frame. But the awkward angle and potential for damage rule out using a hammer. You could go out and buy a brad pusher (a specialized tool used by the pros), but why spend the money? For a handy, shop-made brad pusher, just modify a pair of adjustable pliers. Stick a scrap of mat board on the bottom jaw with some double-faced tape to protect the frame. Simple and cheap.

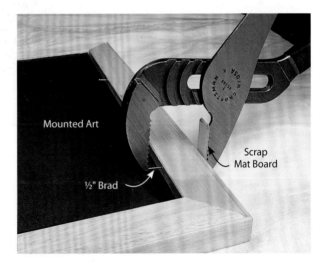

Mounted Art

½" Brad

Scrap Mat Board

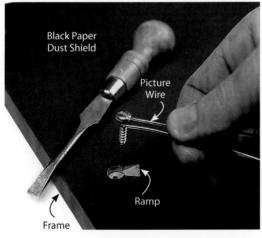

Black Paper Dust Shield

Picture Wire

Ramp

Frame

No-Mar Wire Hangers

Did you ever take down a picture only to find that the hangers have left some nasty scratches on the wall? For a frame that hugs the wall without marring it, try this flush-mount system. Countersink screws into the frame and chisel a ramp out of the hole to avoid kinking the wire. Add bumpers to the lower back of the frame for additional wall protection.

⅛"
Spline   Cut
Flush

Spline Sled

Through-splines are a great way to reinforce miters. They also add a snappy decorative element to any picture frame.

A through-spline is a thin piece of wood that's glued into a slot cut across a miter joint. The spline can be made from contrasting wood for an accent or from the same species for a more subdued effect. Cut and sand the spline flush with the frame edges after the glue has set.

We built this nifty sled for safely cutting the slots for the splines. The picture frame is held in a cradle as the sled rides on your tablesaw fence.

Figure A: Spline Slot Sled
Build the U-shaped guide to fit snugly over your tablesaw fence. Two 2x2 strips are screwed to a 14 in. x 24-in. piece of MDF to form the cradle. A 3-degree bevel on the inside edge of the cradle helps to hold the frame stock securely.

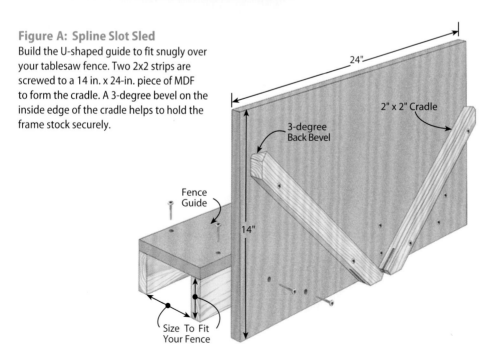

24"

2" x 2" Cradle

3-degree
Back Bevel

Fence
Guide

14"

Size To Fit
Your Fence

CORNER CLAMP FOR BETTER MITERS

by DAVID RADTKE

This shop-made miter clamp has many of the same advantages as the expensive metal ones. It's strong, easy to use, holds project parts both square and flat, and allows you to adjust one part at a time. The slot in the bottom lets you examine the back of your miter to make sure it's properly aligned. It also keeps glue from smearing on the miter's back.

It's simple to make this clamp out of some scrap plywood. Make the center 4-in.-square block from two layers of ¾-in. plywood glued together. Double-check that this block is perfectly square and drill a 2-in. hole in the middle. Make the bottom board 7-in. square, cut the slot with a jigsaw and glue it to the 4-in. block.

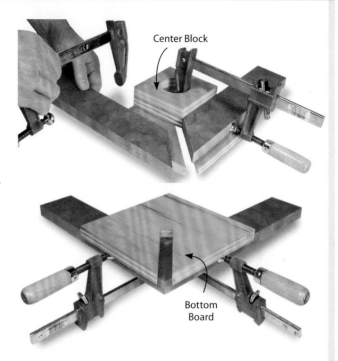

Center Block

Bottom Board

Fingertip Test

To get a mitered frame to come together perfectly two things must happen: (1) the top and bottom must be exactly equal in length; and (2) the two sides must be exactly equal in length. It's natural to want to grab a tape measure to verify these lengths, but forget it. When it comes to checking frame parts for equal length, no tool can come close to your fingertips. Pair up the frame pieces back to back and feel for any ridge where the miters line up. Your fingertip will detect differences smaller than the eye can see or your tape measure can measure.

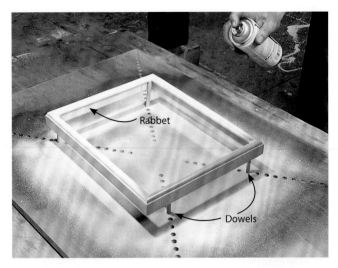

Rabbet

Dowels

Finishing Rack

Here's a neat trick for securely supporting picture frames for finishing. Most frames are too light to hold still while you finish, especially when using a brush-on finish. This simple, easy-to-store finishing rack ends the hassles. Dowels are set in holes drilled diagonally from the corners of a piece of sheet stock. The frame is held firmly in the rack by its own rabbet. Now you can brush or spray almost any size frame with ease.

Quick-Change Fasteners

For some frames, like those with the kids' school photos, removable backs are the best choice. Here's how to make your own quick-change fasteners. Cut ¾-in. fender washers almost in half with a hacksaw. Use a Forstner bit to drill shallow holes in the inside edge of the frame. The bottom of the holes should be slightly below the back of the mounting board. A small hole drilled in the washer makes it easy to open and close the fasteners.

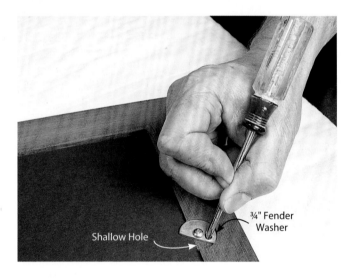

¾" Fender Washer

Shallow Hole

Picture-Perfect Frame Miters

Few things are more frustrating than trying to get good-looking miter joints on all four corners of a picture frame. Three requirements guarantee success: the miters must be right on 45-degrees, the two sides must be exactly equal in length and the top and bottom must be exactly equal in length.

Our miter sled ensures you'll meet all of these requirements. It also offers repeatability, which allows you to quickly cut consistent parts for multiple frames. If you've struggled with making a crosscut sled for your saw, relax. This sled is a cinch to build. Before you start, check your tablesaw to make sure the fence and blade are parallel

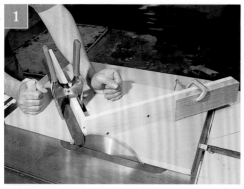

Cut the first miter by clamping the stock on the fence that faces the operator.

Cut the second miter on the opposite fence with the newly mitered end locked into the mitered stop block.

to the miter slot and the blade is 90 degrees to the table. Then follow these steps:

1. Cut a ½-in.-thick hardwood runner so it slides in your miter slot without slop.

2. Run a ¼-in.-deep dado in the bottom of the base. Position the dado so the edge of the base overhangs the saw's line of cut.

3. Glue or screw the runner in place.

4. Once the glue is dry, set the base in the miter slot and trim the overhanging edge. Use the same blade you intend to use for cutting miters. We recommend a high tooth count cross-cut blade.

5. Cut a triangular fence support. It's essential that the apex of the triangle be a perfect 90-degrees.

6. Notch the sides of the support for spring clamps.

7. Fasten the fence support to the base using a combination square to establish the 45-degree angle.

8. Add the fence and handles.

9. Finally, make a hardwood stop-block with a 45-degree angle cut on one end.

**Figure B:
Perfect Miter Sled**

This easy-to-build sled helps cut perfect miters every time.

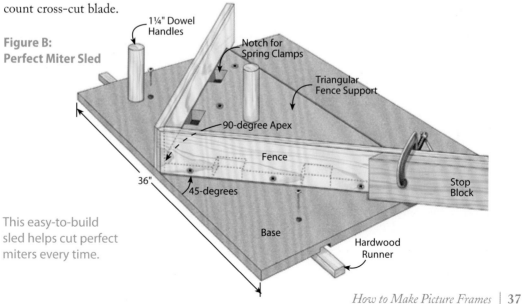

1¼" Dowel Handles

Notch for Spring Clamps

Triangular Fence Support

90-degree Apex

Fence

36"

45-degrees

Stop Block

Base

Hardwood Runner

Four-Point Frame Clamp

This shop-made frame clamp puts equal pressure on all four corners of your frame at once, for quick, hassle-free assembly. Use scraps of paper towel under each joint to absorb glue squeeze out. Set the pivoting corner blocks to fit your frame. Apply enough clamp pressure to hold the frame together but still allow you to align the pieces for a perfect fit. Finally, clamp tight.

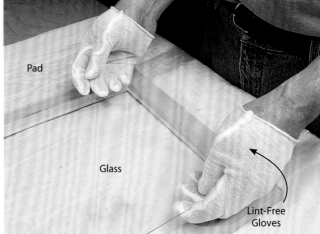

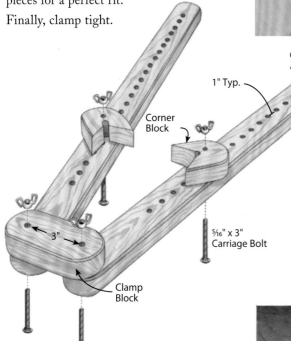

Figure C: Four-Point Frame Clamp
We used hard maple for our clamp, but any hardwood will do. The clamp arms are 1 in. x 2 in. x 30-in. long. The clamp block is 1 in. x 2 in. x 5 in. and the corner blocks are 1 in. x 2 in. x 3½ in. Drill a 5⁄16-in. hole in the center of the corner blocks and cut a 90-degree notch into the hole with a bandsaw. Add a second hole, ¾-in. behind the first, for the carriage bolts. Use eight 5⁄16 in. x 3-in. carriage bolts and wing nuts.

Keep It Clean!

It's essential to work in a clean environment during final assembly. Wear a pair of lint-free darkroom gloves during final assembly to keep fingerprints off the mat and glass. Protect the finished frame with a pad and keep a sharp eye out for dust and debris.

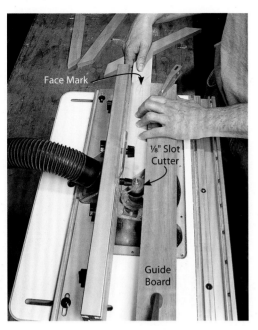

Face Mark

⅛" Slot Cutter

Guide Board

Blind Splines

Until somebody discovers a miracle glue for end grain, miter joints will need reinforcement. Nails work, but pounding them in delicate frame material can be risky. Blind splines offer invisible reinforcement without nails.

Cut the slots on a router table using a guide board and a ⅛-in. slot cutter. Each piece is cut face up (mark the faces as a reminder). Feed the stock from the right for one cut and from the left for the second cut.

Cut the splines from a strip of hardwood with a 1-in. plug cutter and orient the grain perpendicular to the joint for strength.

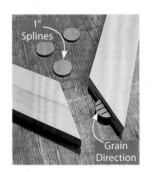

1" Splines

Grain Direction

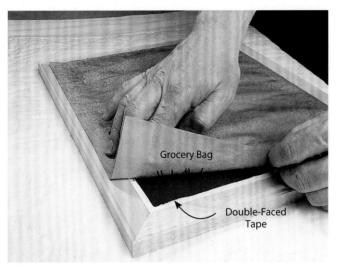

Grocery Bag

Double-Faced Tape

Grocery Bag Dust Shield

Dust and insects have an uncanny knack for finding their way into framed artwork. Professional framers always seal the back of the frame with a paper dust shield. You don't need special paper for this, a plain grocery bag works just fine. (For larger frames, use brown kraft paper available at art supply stores.) Run double-faced tape along the inside edge of the frame and press the paper in place to seal the frame.

Tip For a neater look, dampen the paper with a sponge after taping. The moistened paper will shrink as it dries, leaving a tight, wrinkle-free dust shield to protect your artwork.

by DAVE MUNKITTRICK *and* DAVE RADTKE

Router Moldings

TIPS ON SAFELY MAKING CLEAN-CUT MOLDINGS FOR YOUR HOME AND PROJECTS

Scallop-Free Moldings

Once I bought a router and a tablesaw, I could hardly wait to make new trim moldings for my house. My enthusiasm soon waned as I spent hours sanding out all the unwanted bumps and irregularities caused by uneven hand pressure. After I showed a buddy my raw fingertips, he showed me his featherboards. Wow, what a difference! Now all of my moldings have a clean profile that runs the whole length of the stock.

Featherboards work because unlike you, they never let go. They consistently hold your stock firmly against the fence and the router table for clean, scallop-free moldings.

Featherboards are nothing more than pieces of straight-grained, ¾-in. stock with ¼-in. to ½-in. wide fingers cut in them. The ends are cut square or at an angle. The blunt end provides single-point pressure and can be used at any angle. Angled featherboards apply pressure over a broader area.

Now, I'm cranking out moldings that require little or no sanding.

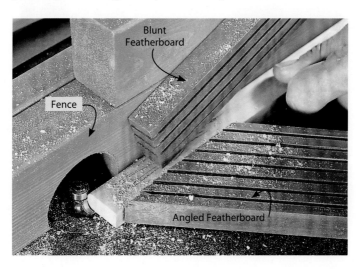

Blunt Featherboard

Fence

Angled Featherboard

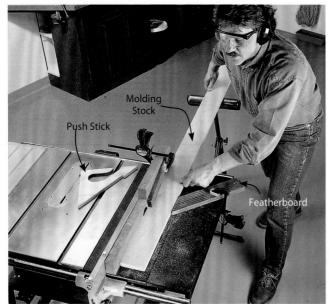

Molding
Stock

Push Stick

Featherboard

Feed Right to Eliminate Burning

Even a brief pause to reposition your hands while feeding stock can result in a nasty burn mark on a strip of molding. Sanding out a burn is a tedious job that you can avoid. The trick is to maintain a steady feed rate. Here's how. Position yourself so you can push the stock all the way through with one continuous motion. Let a pair of featherboards hold the stock while you keep up an even hand-over-hand feed rate. Keep a push stick within easy reach so you can finish the cut without the "pause that burns."

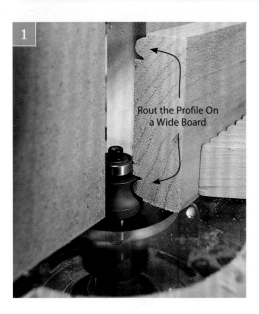

1

Rout the Profile On
a Wide Board

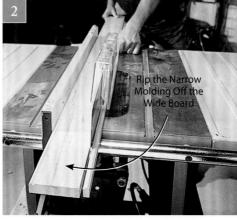

2

Rip the Narrow
Molding Off the
Wide Board

A Safe Way to Cut Small Moldings

It's hard to keep thin stock from chattering while it's being cut on a router table. For narrow strips like this bead molding, it's safer and easier to rout the profile first on a wider board (photo at left), then rip the shaped edge off on the tablesaw (photo above).

Use Oversized Bearings for First Cut

When cutting moldings with a hand-held router, I always take a shallow cut first, then lower the bit for a full-depth cut. I recently bought a molding bit with a profile that wouldn't allow this procedure. The bit was way too big for a single pass and the molding stock was too long to do on my router table. Solution: I fit the bit with a larger bearing to make the first cut. Then I replaced the original bearing for the final cut. Perfect!

Router-Made Bull's-Eye Blocks

A plunge router, a top-bearing classical bit and a couple of holesaws are all you need to make perfect bull's-eyes every time. Use the holesaws to cut the 3½-in. and 1⅝-in. holes in the jig.

You can get four corner blocks from a 4¼-in. by 20-in. board. Mark off each square as shown in the photo. Then use a compass to mark concentric 3½-in. and 1⅝-in. circles at each center. Clamp the jig over the workpiece so the large hole lines up with the large circle on the workpiece. Set your plunge router for a ³⁄₁₆-in.-deep cut. Make a clockwise pass, then set the depth to ⁷⁄₁₆-in. and make the final pass. Next, flip the jig over and align the small hole with the inner ring of the bull's-eye and rout. Repeat the process for all four blocks.

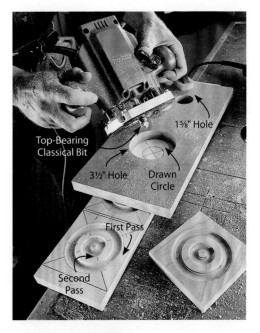

Top-Bearing Classical Bit

1⅝" Hole

3½" Hole

Drawn Circle

First Pass

Second Pass

Routing Fluted Moldings

Routing a fluted molding on a router table or with an edge guide is tricky. One slip (usually on the last flute) and your piece is ruined. This neat jig will have you churning out perfect flutes every time. It can handle stock up to ¹³⁄₁₆-in. thick and 3½-in. wide or modify the design for larger stock.

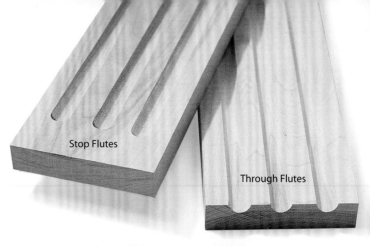

Stop Flutes

Through Flutes

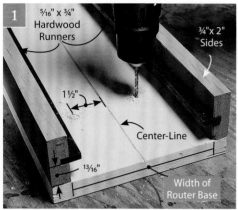

Build the jig to fit your router base exactly. Make a light scoring cut down the middle of the base as a centerline. Lay out and drill holes for the hold-down screws so they fall between the flutes. This avoids any unpleasant contact between the screws and the router bit.

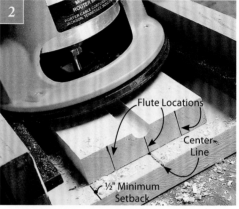

Cut the flutes with a ½-in. core-box bit. Start by marking the flute locations on the ends of your piece, and align the centerline with the center flute mark. Install the hold-down screws and rout the first flute, taking a shallow cut followed by a full-depth cut.

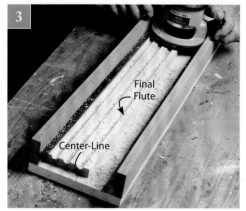

Cut the outside flutes by repositioning the workpiece to the other side of the jig.

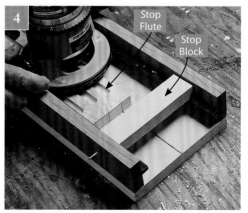

Nail a stop block between the sides of the jig for stop flutes.

Vertical Molding Bits

Are you frustrated with the crummy selection, quality and price of manufactured moldings at your home center? If so, check out the selection of router bits designed so you can make your own moldings. These bits cut on the vertical, not the horizontal, so you don't have huge cutting wings spinning at a million miles an hour. Consequently, these bits are safer to use and don't require a variable-speed router or a 4-in. hole in your router table!

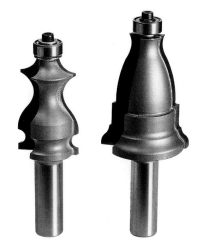

Leave a Handle

Leave a Handle for Safer Routing

When you're cutting delicate moldings and using featherboards it's almost impossible to safely feed the stock all the way through. Don't push your luck and try to finish the cut. Sometimes it's best to waste a little wood and leave some extra stock as a handle on the end for safety. When you've cut as far as possible, turn off the router, remove the piece and cut off the handle.

Perfect Profile Sanding Block

Intricate molding, like this piece, can be a real chore to sand. A sanding block that perfectly matches the profile makes the job a whole lot easier and faster. Here's how to make one. Put plastic wrap over the profile. Make sure the plastic conforms to the profile without any wrinkles. Then mix a two-part auto-body filler and place it on the wrapped section of molding. Fold the extra plastic wrap around the filler and let it harden into a block. In about 30 minutes your block will be ready to use. For wide, intricate profiles like the one shown, you may want to make two narrower blocks that are easier to handle than one wide one.

Auto-body filler is available from auto parts and supplies stores.

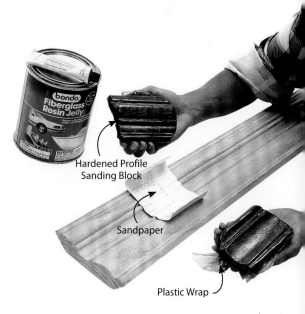

Hardened Profile Sanding Block

Sandpaper

Plastic Wrap

by ERIC SMITH

Three Router-Made Picture Frames

THREE CUSTOM PROFILES WITH INFINITE POSSIBILITIES

Your router table is the perfect tool for making an almost limitless variety of picture frames. The problem is that with so many router bits and possible combinations of bits, where do you start? The three picture-frame profiles in this article are a good beginning. With the exception of the final profile, all use common router bits. Each frame illustrates a basic technique; use them as springboards for your own unique creations.

One-Bit Frames Are Fast and Easy

This mahogany picture frame is no two-bit design. The complete profile is made with a single ⅜-in. rabbeting bit, a single fence setting and a single depth-of-cut setting. There's no fussing around.

Repeating a router-bit cut on both sides of a piece of wood or changing the depth of the cut are easy ways to create unique profiles. Try using different router-bit profiles for other custom frames.

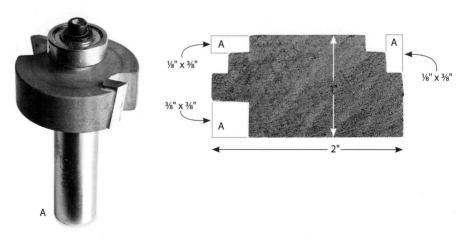

⅛" x ⅜"

⅜" x ⅜"

1"

⅛" x ⅜"

2"

A

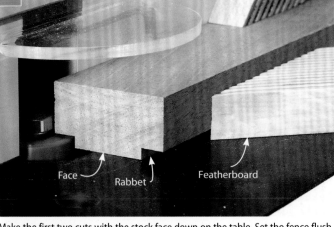

Make the first two cuts with the stock face down on the table. Set the fence flush with the bearing and raise the bit to cut a ⅛-in. x ⅜-in. rabbet. Featherboards guarantee smooth, straight cuts.

Make the second two cuts with the stock on edge. The fence and bit-height settings remain the same.

Make Large Frames in Two Parts

Two-part (or even three- or four-part) frames are a great way to create deep, eye-catching picture frames beefy enough for a big landscape painting but capable of holding even a small family photo.

I built this frame with cherry on the outside and quartersawn sycamore in the inside. Make the inner frame first, cutting the usual ⅜-in. rabbet (Photo 1) and then routing the profile on the face (Photo 2).

Then machine the outside frame (Photos 3 through 6). Miter and glue the inner frame; then cut the outer frame to fit. Tack the frames together with a few brad nails.

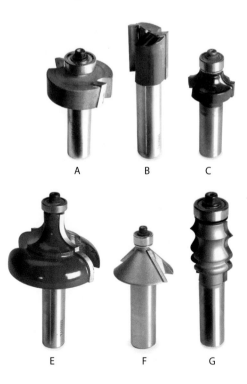

A   B   C

E   F   G

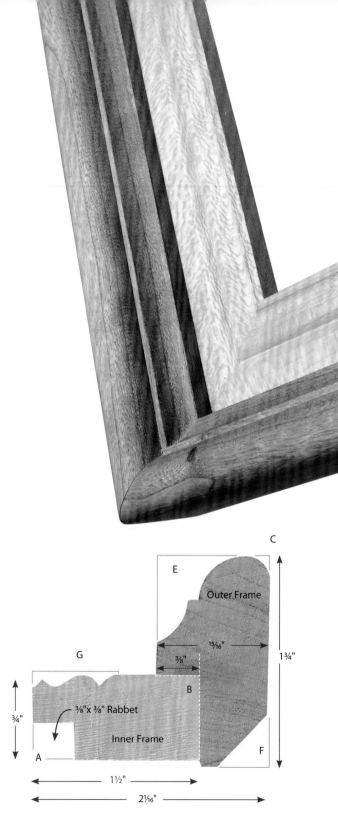

Outer Frame

¹⁵⁄₁₆"

⅜"

1¾"

G

¾"

⅜" x ⅜" Rabbet

Inner Frame

B

F

A

1½"

2¹⁄₁₆"

C

E

1

On the inner frame, cut the rabbet to house the matte board, glass and artwork.

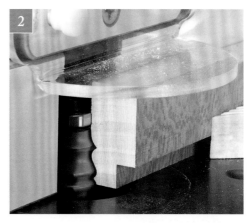

2

Add a distinctive profile to the face of the inner frame using a specialized picture-frame molding bit.

3

The outer frame gets an ogee profile. I used a specialized bit that creates an extra-large roundover.

4

Complete the rounded edge by flipping the board and routing a roundover on the ogee's opposite side.

5

Use a straight bit to cut a rabbet to house the inner frame.

6

Chamfer the back edge to lift the frame off the wall and make the frame appear less massive.

Inlays Add Interest and Depth

Make this frame profile using three standard router bits: a ¼-in. round-over bit, a classic ogee bit and a ¾-in. straight bit. Rout all of the pieces, glue the inlay, and then cut the miters. I like to use contrasting woods, in this case, riftsawn white oak with a purpleheart inlay.

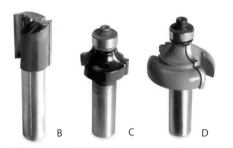

B   C   D

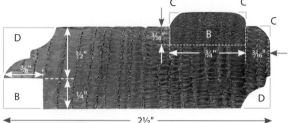

C   C   C

D   B   ³⁄₁₆"   ³⁄₁₆"

½"   ¾"

³⁄₈"

B   ¼"   D

2½"

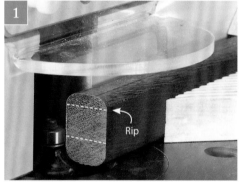

1 Round all four edges on an extra-wide blank of inlay stock. Make the blank at least 1½ in. wide so you can safely rip two ⅜-in.-deep inlays from each blank.

2 Rout the roundover on the outside edge of the frame stock.

3 Plow the inlay groove next to the rounded edge.

4 Cut the inside edge profile using a classic ogee bit. Cut the back edge profile by dropping the bit to half height. Move the fence forward to cut half the bit's depth.

Frame Clamp

by RICK BAIRD

Two triangular maple blocks and a pair of sharp-tipped drywall screws are all you need to make corner clamp blocks for picture frames.

Drill and counterbore a hole for a drywall screw through one leg of each block, positioned so the screw's tip is centered in the hypotenuse (photo, below). Make sure the screw threads through the shank hole, so you can turn it in and out. For hard woods, extend the screws so their tips barely protrude; extend the tips a bit further for soft woods.

To use the blocks, assemble the joint, with one frame side clamped to your bench. Press a clamp block to each side. When you clamp across the joint, the screw tips bite in and keep the blocks from sliding. The screws leave small dimples, which can be easily taken care of with wood filler or a few drops of water to raise the grain. To accommodate joint angles other than 45 degrees, simply modify the shape of the blocks.

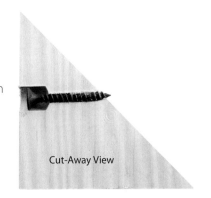

Cut-Away View

by ERIC SMITH *and* RICHARD TENDICK

Tablesaw Picture Frame

SAFELY MAKE SHAPER-QUALITY MOLDING ON YOUR TABLESAW WITHOUT FANCY JIGS

This how-to story has a picture-perfect ending. In fact, you might want to round up some spectators for applause in the final steps. Richard Tendick has developed a safe, simple technique to help you make narrow, complex picture-frame stock using nothing more than a tablesaw. That's right, there are no routers or specialized jigs and sleds to make, either. With Richard's system, you actually glue the frame before the final cut. The fun comes when the frame is cut loose from the square stock.

Richard's molding also simplifies assembly. Mitering and gluing odd-shaped picture frame molding can be a struggle. With this technique, the frame is mitered and glued when the stock still has its square profile. That makes building a picture frame much easier.

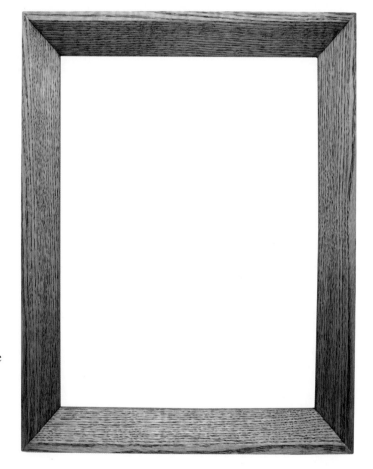

Figure A: Picture Frame Profile Cuts

Five rip cuts create the picture frame profile. The first four cuts are made with most of the 1½-in. square piece still intact. That means plenty of wood is riding against the tablesaw bed and fence—no rocking or pinching to worry about as you push the stock through. When you plan your cuts, make sure the face of the frame is cut roughly perpendicular to the growth rings. This yields straight grain that flows smoothly from miter to miter.

Note: All profiles are shown from the outfeed end of the saw. For this project, we used a right-tilt tablesaw with the fence moved to the left of the blade. Reverse all diagrams for a left-tilt saw.

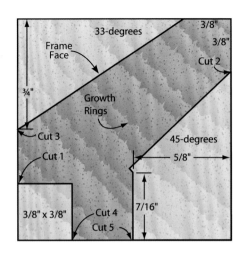

Cut 1

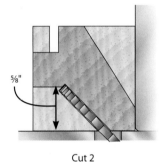

Cut 2

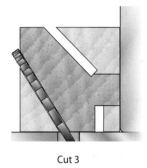

Cut 3

PROJECT REQUIREMENTS AT A GLANCE

Materials:
- 1½-in. square oak stair balusters
- Band clamp

Tools:
- Tablesaw
- Stock miter gauge
- Drill
- Sander

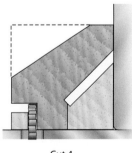

Cut 4

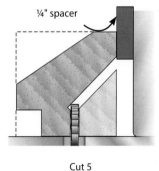

Cut 5

Grain and Color are Important

This technique requires 1½-in. square stock. For a frame to look good, the grain must flow smoothly around all four pieces (see "Oops," below), and the color must be consistent. Choose clear, straight-grained wood for your frame stock. It's best if you can cut the frame stock from a single length of wood. Buy extra wood for test cuts. We found 1½-in. square oak stair balusters sold at home centers to be an excellent source for frame stock.

Set Up for the Cuts

1. Rough-cut the frame stock to a few inches over the finished dimensions for cutting on the tablesaw.

2. Sketch the cuts on the end of each piece for orientation (Photo 1; Fig. A). All cuts start at the same end, so if you find yourself reversing the piece, something is wrong. Pay attention to grain direction! (See Fig. A and "Oops.")

3. Cut spacer strips ⅜, ⅝ and ¾ in. wide by 18 in. long. You'll use these for setting the fence and saw blade height for some of the cuts.

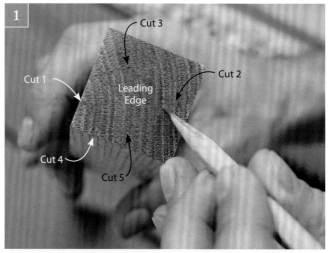

Sketch the saw cuts on the leading end (the end that goes into the saw blade first) of the frame stock before you start cutting.

Oops!

At first we didn't pay attention to grain orientation. The result was mismatched grain and a bad-looking corner. Make sure the face of your frame is positioned so the growth rings run perpendicular to it. This will give you a straight-grained face, which will make the corners match better.

Straight Grain Face

Tip

Get a Better Grip
Hold small pieces of wood in the tablesaw with this rubber-tipped push stick. Just glue a standard eraser into the push stick notch.

Rubber Eraser

Use spacer sticks to set the fence and blade height for Cut 2. With the blade at 45 degrees, use the ⅜-in. spacer to set the fence. When the teeth center on the ⅝-in. spacer's upper corner, you've reached the blade height.

Caution! The guard is removed for this operation.

Tilt the blade 33 degrees to make Cut 3. Use a ¾-in. spacer to set the fence. A featherboard and a rubber-tipped push stick make the cut smooth and safe.

Caution! The guard is removed for this operation.

Make Cut 4 on the side of the blade away from the fence to prevent kickback. This also allows the stock's large sides to bear against the fence and table for greater stability.

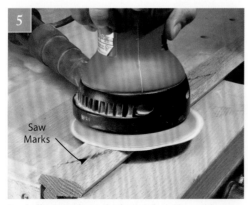

Sand off saw marks on the frame's face. The molding can be pinched in a vise to hold it steady.

Making the Saw Cuts

4. Set the blade to make a ⅜-in.-deep cut and make Cut 1 (Fig. A).

5. Set the blade and fence for Cut 2 (Photo 2) and make the cut.

6. Make Cut 3 with the blade tilted to 33 degrees. Set the blade just high enough to poke through the wood about ¼ in. (Photo 3).

7. Make Cut 4 to create the rabbet that holds your picture, matte and glass (Photo 4). Set the fence and blade height using Cut 1 as a reference.

Sanding, Mitering and Gluing

8. Sand the frame before cutting the miters (Photo 5). It's a lot easier than sanding into the corners of an assembled frame.

9. Before you cut the miters, take a ½-in.-thick slice off your stock. Save the slice for setting up the last cut.

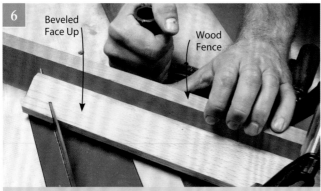

6   Beveled Face Up   Wood Fence

Caution! The guard is removed for this operation.

Make the first miter cuts to the left of the blade. Clamp the stock face up to a wooden fence attached to the gauge. The end being cut should angle toward you. Make this cut on all four pieces.

7   Stop Block

Caution! The guard is removed for this operation.

Make the second miter cut on the right side of the blade. Clamp a stop block to the fence so the frame's parallel sides will be exactly the same length.

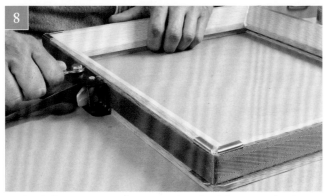

8

Glue and clamp the mitered frame together. A band clamp is perfect for the job. The clamp's metal plates hang on each corner of the frame to help position the band and protect the wood.

10. Attach a long subfence to the miter gauge. Use a drafting square to set the gauge at 45 degrees.

11. Cut the miters (Photos 6 and 7).

12. Test-fit the frame with a band clamp before gluing, to check for tight-fitting joints.

13. Glue the frame together, spreading a heavy coat of glue over the entire miter (Photo 8). Yes, that includes the part that will eventually be cut off. Wipe off excess glue with a damp rag.

The Final Cut (The Fun Part!)

14. Set up the tablesaw for Cut 5 (Photo 9).

15. Make the final cut on all four sides of the frame (Photo 10).

16. Lift the frame from its four-sided offcut (Photo 11). (You may want an audience for this step.)

9   ¼" Spacer Board   Offcut   1⅛"

Set up your tablesaw for the final cut using a cross section of the frame stock as a guide. Clamp a ¼-in. spacer to the fence just above the offcut to create a gap between the offcut and the fence to prevent kickback.

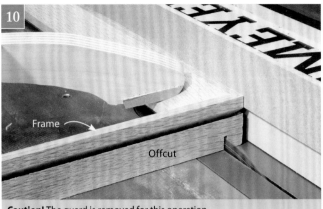

Caution! The guard is removed for this operation.

Make Cut 5 on all four sides of the frame. The offcut won't release from the frame until all the cuts are complete.

Lift the frame out of the offcut. If your last cut was a bit shallow, you may need to push down in spots to separate the frame from the offcut.

Drill pilot holes for a couple of 1-in. brads to reinforce each miter joint. Keep the brads on the back of the frame where they won't be seen.

17. If the inner frame doesn't fall away from the offcut immediately, don't panic. Ours didn't (and of course, we panicked). It turned out that despite our best efforts, the blade was set a hair too shallow. All we had to do was push down gently on the frame to break that sliver of wood and release the offcut.

Finishing Touches

18. Reinforce the corners with 1-in. wire brads (Photo 12). Predrill the holes with a No. 60 wire gauge bit or clip the head off a brad and use that as a bit. You may need to use a mini-chuck if your drill doesn't hold a bit that small. We don't recommend using a nail gun for this step—it's too easy to blow a nail out of the face of the frame. The nail would be hard to extract, and the resulting damage, difficult to repair. With a drill, if you accidentally drill a hole in the wrong spot, it's easy to hide with filler.

19. Sand the outside of the frame and fill the nail holes. Stain as desired and finish with at least two coats of varnish or polyurethane.

HARVEY PENICK'S
LITTLE RED BOOK
Stahlkuppe GREAT DANES
Stahlkuppe Great Danes
TOM

Picture Frame Projects

N ow that you have learned many of the technical aspects of frame construction, it's time to explore creative options for your picture frames. And there are many.

Begin with a rustic frame created from found wood and proceed to oval frames that are easier to make than you might believe. Or, how about creating a personalized photograph album featuring a personalized wooden binding for a special friend or family member? That gift will be cherished, remembered, and used for years to come.

This section also explores the myriad of frames that can be built completely without corners and will accentuate anyone's home décor. The easy-to-follow instructions, photographs, and illustration contained here will correctly guide you through a process that should spark your creative energies in completely new directions.

If your tastes run in a more eclectic direction, there is a collection of fantastic and fabulous frames that should serve as a gateway for you to express your individual artistic vision.

Lastly, for traditionalists, there are also frames built using half-lap joints, and hallway mirror projects constructed from oak or sycamore.

Whatever projects you choose, and whether you build them for yourself or for others, this collection of American Woodworker magazine frame projects will help you learn to harness your creative spirit and create some truly amazing wood projects.

edited by DAVE MUNKITTRICK

Rustic Picture Frame

FOUND WOOD BRINGS OUTSTANDING RESULTS

Picture this: your favorite family photo in a frame made of wood harvested from your own backyard. Believe it or not, there are some real diamonds in the rough to be found in firewood or even fallen limbs, and the best part of all—it's free! Turning logs into lumber is a lot of fun. Logs 6-in. or more in diameter are best. Accept a certain degree of defect in the wood and if a piece doesn't work out or you blow it the first time through, no big deal. You can never have too much kindling!

Prepare the Stock

First, run the flat of the log on your jointer to create a reference surface for sawing the log on the bandsaw (Photo 1). Then, create a 90-degree edge to use against the fence of your bandsaw. Mark each piece in the order it comes off the log. This helps you orient the grain when you build the frame. Chances are the wood will need to dry, so sticker your best pieces indoors and let them dry. Use a moisture meter and test for a moisture content of around 8 percent before using your wood.

Build the Frame

Once your wood is dry you can start to build the picture frame. Joint and plane each piece to a uniform thickness. On the bandsaw, rip the pieces down so they are somewhat equal in width. Then joint the inside edges so they can register against the fence of a miter box. Cut miters on all the ends. With a bark edge,

Slice up a log before you burn it. You may find buried treasure!

it's hard to take precise measurements, so a little bit of trial and error is required to get good miters on all four corners.

Dry fit the frame and even up the inside edges (Photo 2). Cut the inside edge profile on the bandsaw and sand it smooth.

You'll have to cut a rabbet on the back of the frame to hold your picture. Use a router table and a rabbeting bit set deep enough to accommodate glass, matting, picture, and backing (approx. ⅜ in.).

Assembly

Glue one joint at a time using a quick-setting glue like Titebond's Wood Molding Glue. To avoid damaging the bark edge, use the specialized clamps featured in Photo 3.

Sand and finish the frame. Attach screw eyes and picture wire. Mount the picture and hang it on a wall near your fireplace for all to enjoy.

Saw the log into 1-in.-thick slices. After each cut, joint the edge of the log to smooth the face of the next piece. Set the slices aside to dry.

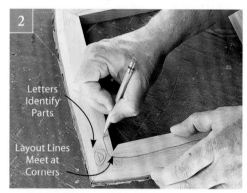

Mark inside edges for trimming, while holding the outer edges flush at the corners. You can shoot for a perfectly straight inside edge or follow the grain for a more natural look. Letter each miter joint for easy identification.

Clamp the joints with the most versatile clamps in your shop, your hands. Usually a few minutes of hand pressure results in a good initial tack set. Let the glue cure a good half-hour before moving on to the next joint. Tip: A piece of waxed paper under the joint keeps the frame from sticking to your bench.

by RANDY JOHNSON

Oval Picture Frames

DON'T LET THEIR SHAPE INTIMIDATE YOU—JIGS MAKE CLASSIC FRAMES EASY

Oval frames are delightful eye-catchers, evoking images of days gone by and giving a unique setting for that very special photo. At first glance these frames may look tricky, but we've figured out an easy way to make them. You don't even have to know how to draw an oval. Simple-to-make jigs and patterns are all it takes. In fact, this method can be used to make almost any size oval or round frame.

Oval Frames in Four Easy Steps

The four basic steps to making an oval frame are:

1. Create a frame pattern using a piece of oval glass, some ¼-in. plywood, and a couple of washers (Fig. C and Photos 1 through 5).

2. Prepare the frame parts for routing. This involves cutting the miters to size, gluing them together, and rough sawing the oval shape (Fig. B and Photos 6 through 9).

3. Make the router jigs and rout the frame to final size and shape (Figs. A, E, F, G and H and Photos 10 through 13).

4. Finish your frame and install the glass, mat, picture, and an oval screw ring, and it's ready for the wall.

Materials and Tools

It takes only 2 bd. ft. of 1⅛-in.-thick lumber to make one of the frames shown here. The jigs can be built from scrap ¾-in. plywood or medium-density fiberboard (MDF). You can buy oval glass from a picture-frame shop online. Your local framing shop should be able to make you an oval mat. You can also cut your own glass and mat and save money (see "Cutting Your Own Ovals", page 71).

The tools you need to build the jigs and frame are a tablesaw, a jigsaw, a router with a ½-in. collet, and a drill press with a drum-sander attachment. You will also need a flush trim rabbet, 45-degree chamfer, a Roman-ogee router bit, and a slot cutter. If your lumber is rough sawn you'll need a planer and jointer. A router table and either a belt sander or disc sander are also handy but not absolutely necessary.

Router Table vs. Router Jigs

There are a couple of steps (Photos 12 and 13) that can be done on a router table or with the frame-holding jigs (Figs. G and H). I opted for the jigs because I think they're safer and easier to use. When I tried making these cuts on the router table, I found holding the frame with push blocks awkward because they tended to slip off the narrow frame during routing. I did use the router table to cut the spline slots (Photo 6) because it's quick and accurate, but the slots could just as well be cut on the tablesaw.

We designed this frame for an 8x10 photo without a mat or a smaller photo with a mat, but you can make the jigs bigger or smaller to fit almost any size photo.

Figure A: Oval Frame Cross Section
The shape of the oval frame is created with the use of four different router bits; a flush-trim for routing the frame to width, a chamfer, a rabbet and a Roman-ogee.

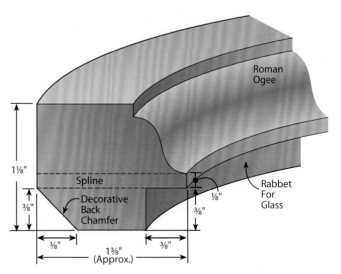

Roman Ogee

Spline

Rabbet For Glass

Decorative Back Chamfer

1⅛"

⅜"

⅛"

⅜"

⅜"

1⅜"
(Approx.)

⅜"

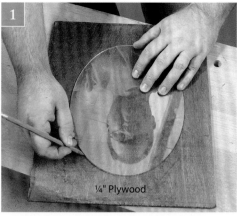

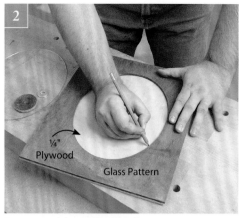

Start with your oval glass and trace it onto a piece of ¼-in. plywood. Then saw out the inside with a jigsaw and carefully drum sand right up to the pencil line. This piece of plywood is your glass pattern.

Trace around the inside of the glass pattern onto another piece of ¼-in. plywood. This new piece of plywood will become your actual frame pattern (Fig. C).

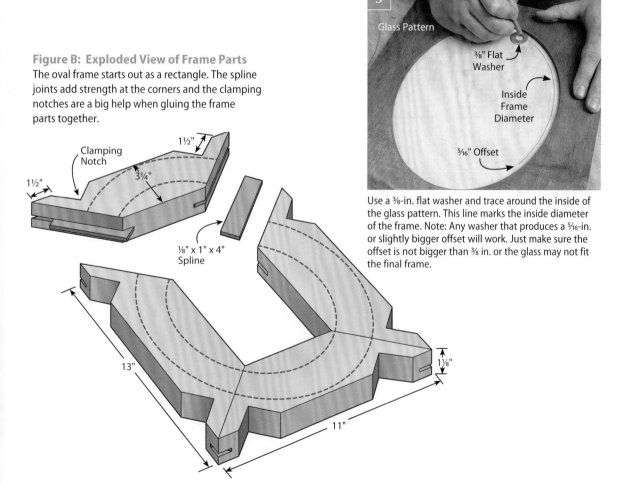

Use a ⅜-in. flat washer and trace around the inside of the glass pattern. This line marks the inside diameter of the frame. Note: Any washer that produces a ⁵⁄₁₆-in. or slightly bigger offset will work. Just make sure the offset is not bigger than ⅜ in. or the glass may not fit the final frame.

Figure B: Exploded View of Frame Parts

The oval frame starts out as a rectangle. The spline joints add strength at the corners and the clamping notches are a big help when gluing the frame parts together.

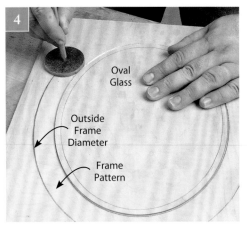

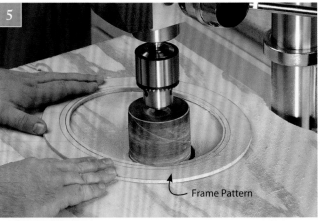

Draw around the glass using a 2⅛-in.-dia. plywood disc. This marks the outside diameter of your frame. Use your oval glass as a guide by centering it on the line you drew earlier (Photo 2).

Complete the frame pattern by cutting it out and sanding it to final size. Leave the inside and outside diameter pencil lines. Be careful to sand the oval evenly, without any lumps or valleys.

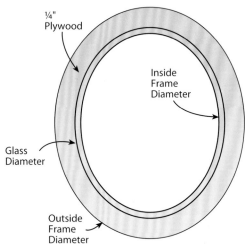

Rout the spline slots in the mitered ends of your frame parts (Fig. D). Next make the splines. They should slip easily into the slots, but without a lot of play.

Figure C: Oval Frame Pattern
Make this out of ¼-in. plywood.
Photos 1 through 5 show you how.

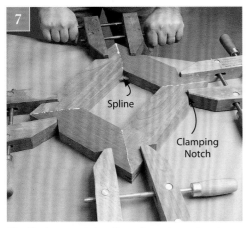

Glue the frame parts together using a clamp at each corner. Use light clamping pressure at first. Increase the pressure once all the parts are correctly aligned. Wipe off any glue squeeze-out while it is still wet or scrape it off later.

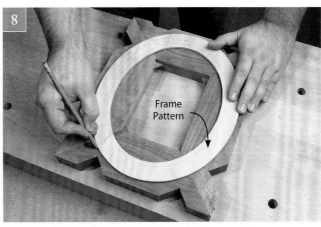

Draw around the inside and outside of your frame pattern. The pattern doesn't need to be perfectly centered on the frame material. Just make sure you have a little extra wood all the way around the outside and inside.

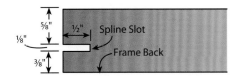

Figure D: Position of Spline Slot
The spline slot is located slightly toward the back of the frame. This keeps the spline from showing up in the Roman ogee (Fig. A).

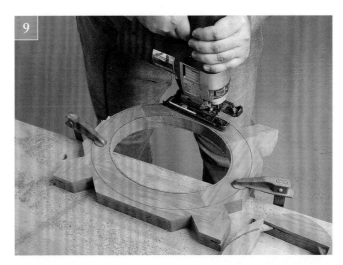

Rough cut the glued-up frame with a jigsaw. Leave about ⅛-in. extra wood beyond the pencil lines.

Flush-trim the inside of the frame using a top-bearing, flush-trim router bit. The rough-cut frame is held to the jig during routing with two screws driven into the back of the frame. The jig is held in the vise by a plywood cleat on the bottom of the jig (Fig. E). If you are only making one or two frames, you could just sand the inside flush using a drumsander and skip making the jig.

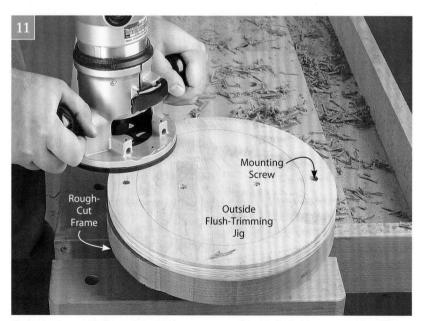

Flush-trim the outside frame diameter the same as you did with the inside, except with a different jig (Fig. F). We experienced some chipping when routing a mahogany frame (see Oops!, page 70), but the walnut we used for the frame shown here routed cleanly.

Figure E: Flush-Trim Jig for Inside Diameter
Attach the rough-cut frame to this jig with two
1¼-in. screws set back ⅝ in. from the inside edge.

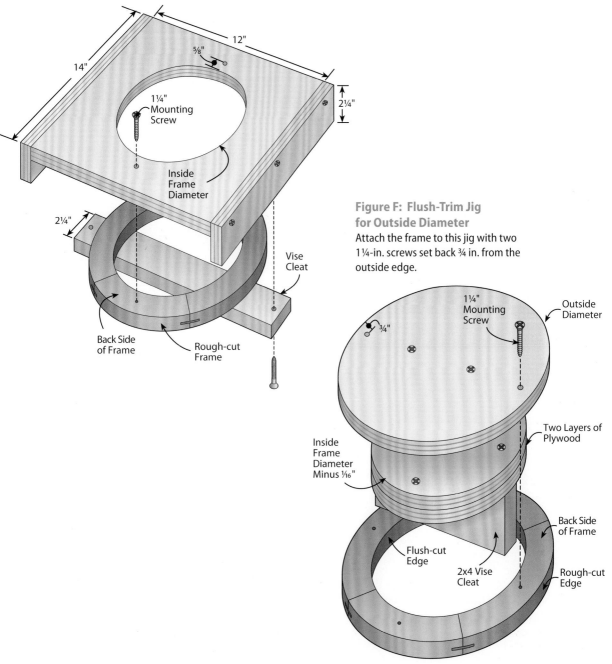

12"

⅝"

14"

1¼"
Mounting
Screw

2¼"

Inside
Frame
Diameter

2¼"

Vise
Cleat

Back Side
of Frame

Rough-cut
Frame

**Figure F: Flush-Trim Jig
for Outside Diameter**
Attach the frame to this jig with two
1¼-in. screws set back ¾ in. from the
outside edge.

1¼"
Mounting
Screw

Outside
Diameter

¾"

Two Layers of
Plywood

Inside
Frame
Diameter
Minus ¹⁄₁₆"

Back Side
of Frame

Flush-cut
Edge

2x4 Vise
Cleat

Rough-cut
Edge

Figure G: Inside Frame-Holding Jig
Use this jig when routing the chamfer on the back of the frame (Photo 12).

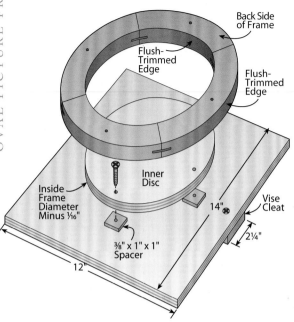

- Back Side of Frame
- Flush-Trimmed Edge
- Flush-Trimmed Edge
- Inner Disc
- Inside Frame Diameter Minus 1/16"
- ⅜" x 1" x 1" Spacer
- 14"
- Vise Cleat
- 2¼"
- 12"

- Inner Disc
- Chamfer
- Inside Frame-Holding Jig

Rout a chamfer on the back outside corner of the flush-trimmed frame. Use the inside frame-holding jig (Fig. G). No screws are needed to hold the frame to this jig, because the inner disc keeps the frame in place.

Oops!

While developing this project we used several types of wood: oak, pine, walnut and mahogany. They all machined nicely except the mahogany. It had a tendency to chip out when flush-trimming the outside diameter. With a curved shape like this you're guaranteed to be routing against the grain somewhere along the edge, making chip-out likely.

If you do experience chip-out, the solution is to sand the outside diameter of the frames rather than rout them. You'll have to do the sanding freehand without the aid of a jig but it does the trick and is almost as fast as routing. So if the wood you choose gives you trouble with chipping, give your belt or disc sander a try.

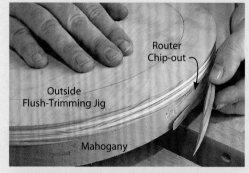

- Router Chip-out
- Outside Flush-Trimming Jig
- Mahogany

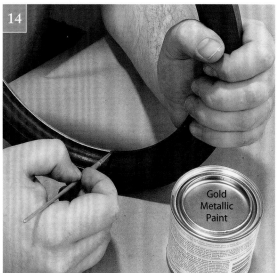

Rout the rabbet for the glass in the back of the frame. This time use the outside holding jig (Fig. H). No screws are needed here either. This jig alone will hold the frame in place while routing. Then flip the frame over and rout the Roman ogee on the front inside edge. When you're done routing, sand the frame and you're ready for finishing.

Finish your frames with your favorite finish. We added a little sparkle to our frames by painting the inside edge with gold metallic paint. You can now install the glass, mat and photo.

Figure H: Outside Frame-Holding Jig

Use this jig when routing the rabbet for the glass and the Roman ogee.

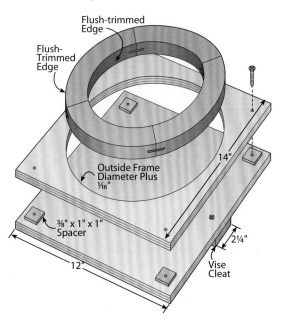

Cutting Your Own Ovals

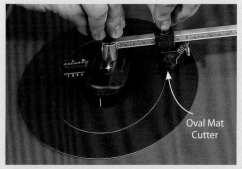

You can buy oval glass and mats or you can make your own. If you want to make them yourself you'll need to purchase two cutters, but they pay for themselves after about a half dozen frames. These cutters cut ovals from as small as 4¼ in. by 7¼ in. to as large as 21½ in. by 24½ in. They produce excellent results and are easy and fun to use.

by DAVE MUNKITTRICK

Photo Album

CREATING BEAUTIFUL, INDIVIDUALIZED DISPLAY PIECES

Do you have a pile of photos waiting to be put in an album? We all do. That's why you can't go wrong making these distinctive photo albums for yourself or as gifts.

Figured wood makes an attractive cover. The first album in the photo was made from a 3 in. x 20 in. piece of tiger maple and the second from a single 6 in. x 10 in. piece of walnut. You can make larger covers (12½ in. x 12½ in.), but they are more likely to warp. The walnut was resawn to make front and back covers. The maple was resawn and glued up to create book-matched covers.

The 9¼ in. x 5 in. acid-free paper pages come pre-drilled and are available from paper suppliers and department or office supply stores. The 2 in. x 24 in. continuous hinge and the brass barrel bolt connectors and screws are available from department, arts and crafts, and office supply stores.

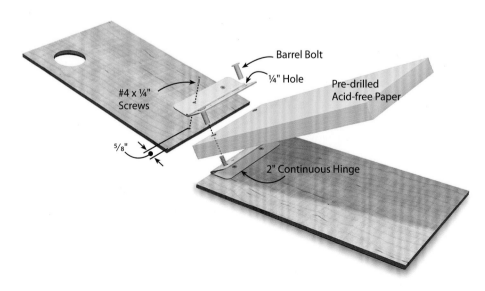

Barrel Bolt

¼" Hole

Pre-drilled Acid-free Paper

#4 x ¼" Screws

⁵⁄₈"

2" Continuous Hinge

How To Make It

1. Surface the covers to about ¼ in. and chamfer the outside edges. (Optional: Use a 1½-in. hole saw to cut a circular frame in the cover.)

2. Sand and finish. We used a sealer coat of Super Blonde Shellac followed by two coats of water-borne polyurethane.

3. Cut two 4-in. lengths of hinge (two 11-in. lengths for 12½ in. x 12½ in. covers) for each album and file a radius on the corners.

4. Use the pre-drilled paper as a template to drill two ¼-in. holes in one leaf of each hinge. File any rough edges smooth.

5. Drill two ⁵⁄₆₄-in. pilot holes ⅝-in. in from the back edge of each cover. Mount the hinges to the cover with #4 screws. (Nip off the ends of the screws if your covers are ¼-in. thick or less.)

6. Bolt the loose leaves of the hinges through the paper with the barrel bolts; add photos and enjoy.

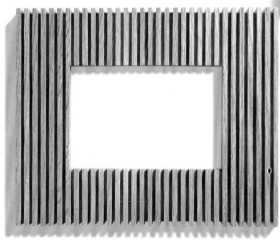

by TIM JOHNSON

Three One-Day Picture Frames

DISTINCTIVE CREATIONS WITHOUT MITERED CORNERS

Mitered corner joints define most picture frames—but not these! The Framed Frame (top left) goes together with half-laps, the Magnetic Frame (middle) employs butt joints and the Grooved Frame (bottom) is simply edge-glued. These distinctive frames share another common trait—they're routed. All three frames are made using a router table; the Framed Frame also requires a small hand-held router. Most of the routing is done with different types of straight bits (flush trim pattern bits and a spiral bit). You'll also need a slot cutter.

You can make any one of these frames in less than a day. They're all made from ¾-in.-thick boards—at most, you'll need a couple board feet per frame. Simple jigs and fixtures make each frame a perfect candidate for making multiples, so they could also be a great solution for your scrap stock problem.

Pro-Quality Stand. The EaselMate frame stand screws on in a minute and can be adjusted to any angle. Available from Albin Products Inc., www.albinproducts.com, 800-225-6821.

Framed Frame

This frame consists of four pieces that are identical except for length (Fig. A). Each piece has two rabbets for the half-lap corner joints, one on each face. The pieces assemble "elephant" style (nose-to-tail). The framed edges are created prior to assembly, by routing away the center of each piece, using a custom-made jig (Fig. B).

You can make a simple version of this frame from a single piece of solid stock that's 2-in.-wide by 36-in.-long. Just plane it to final thickness and you're ready to cut the four pieces. To create the two-tone version shown here, start with three pieces of ¾-in. by 2-in. by 18-in. stock. Glue the pieces together with the contrasting piece in the middle. Resaw the blank in half (Photo 1). Then plane the resawn blanks to final thickness. Each blank contains two frame pieces, one long side and one short side. Cut the four pieces to final size. Then cut the rabbets on each piece (Photo 2).

Plane the center-routing jig's solid wood spacers to ⁹⁄₁₆-in.—the same thickness as the frame pieces. During assembly, center one frame piece between the side spacers. The frame piece must fit snugly. Install the support block. Add the guide pieces, making sure they overhang the frame piece equally, by ³⁄₁₆-in., the width of the framed edges. Slide each frame piece into the jig. After routing and squaring the corners (Photo 3), use the finger notch to grip the piece and remove it.

Dry-assemble the frame and mark the inside edges of each piece. Use a straight bit to rout rabbets for the glass (Photo 4 and Fig. C). Fit one corner joint at a time when you glue the frame together (Photo 5). Clamping the frame between cauls assures a flat result.

Routing creates framed edges more easily than gluing on tiny strips.

Create two-tone blanks for the frame pieces by resawing a lamination of ¾-in.-thick boards. Plane the cherry faces to ³⁄₁₆-in. thickness. Then plane the maple faces until the stock reaches final thickness.

Saw rabbets for the half-lap joints on both ends of each piece. One rabbet goes on the top face; the other goes on the bottom face.

Center Routing

Create the framed edges by routing each piece, using the jig and a mortising bit (at right). Rout just deep enough to remove the top layer of wood. After routing, square the corners with a chisel.

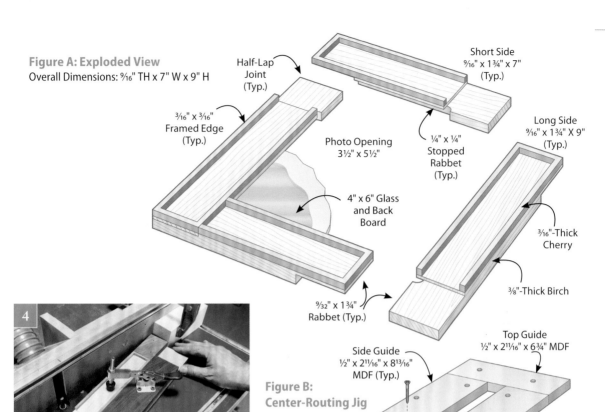

Figure A: Exploded View
Overall Dimensions: ⁹⁄₁₆" TH x 7" W x 9" H

Half-Lap Joint (Typ.)

Short Side
⁹⁄₁₆" x 1¾" x 7"
(Typ.)

³⁄₁₆" x ³⁄₁₆"
Framed Edge
(Typ.)

Photo Opening
3½" x 5½"

¼" x ¼"
Stopped Rabbet
(Typ.)

Long Side
⁹⁄₁₆" x 1¾" X 9"
(Typ.)

4" x 6" Glass
and Back
Board

³⁄₁₆"-Thick
Cherry

³⁄₈"-Thick Birch

⁹⁄₃₂" x 1¾"
Rabbet (Typ.)

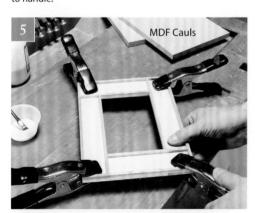

Rout stopped rabbets for the glass. Create clearance for the glass's square corners by making the rabbets extra long. A sled makes the short, narrow frame pieces easier to handle.

MDF Cauls

Clamp the joints with spring clamps for a couple of minutes, until the glue tacks. Then switch to adjustable clamps and re-clamp the frame between MDF cauls, to distribute clamping pressure evenly across the joints.

Figure B: Center-Routing Jig

Side Guide
½" x 2¹¹⁄₁₆" x 8¹³⁄₁₆"
MDF (Typ.)

Top Guide
½" x 2¹¹⁄₁₆" x 6¾" MDF

Support Block
⁹⁄₃₂" x 1⁵⁄₈" x 1¾"

Side Spacer
⁹⁄₁₆" x 2½" x 9"
Solid Wood (typ.)

Top Spacer
⁹⁄₁₆" x 2½" x 6"
Solid Wood

1¾" x 9"
Channel

Base
½" x 6¾" x 11½" MDF

1½"-dia.
Finger Notch

Figure C: Rabbet-Routing Sled

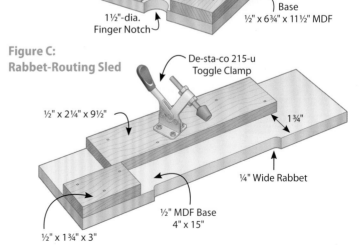

De-sta-co 215-u
Toggle Clamp

½" x 2¼" x 9½"

1¾"

¼" Wide Rabbet

½" MDF Base
4" x 15"

½" x 1¾" x 3"

Magnetic Frame

This frame consists of four identical corner sections that assemble around the glass, photo and back board (Fig. D). Rare earth magnets hold the sections together. To make this frame, you'll need a routing jig (Fig. E), a pattern and two pieces of ¾-in. (or thicker) stock cut to 4¹⁄₁₆-in. by 4⁹⁄₁₆-in. rectangles.

Build the routing jig first. It's used to rout the inside edge of each piece as well as the grooves that house the photo assembly. Use the jig to make the pattern. Saw a 3¹⁄₁₆-in. by 4¹⁄₁₆-in. piece of ½-in. MDF into an L-shape. Install it in the jig and rout the inside edges with a 1-in.-dia. pattern bit (a flush-trim bit with the bearing mounted above the cutting flutes).

Use the pattern to lay out the frame pieces on the two blanks (Photo 1). Cut the short legs to length (Photo 2). Then cut the blanks apart on the bandsaw, install them in the jig and rout the inside edges

(Photos 3 and 4). Install a ³⁄₁₆-in.-wide slot cutter and rout a ½-in. deep slot for the photo assembly (glass, photo and back board) in each piece (Photo 5). The photo assembly provides the frame's structure, so it must fit the slot snugly, but without binding. Size the slot's width to fit the thickness of your photo assembly (for single-strength glass and a ⅛-in. back board, the slot will be slightly less than ¼-in.-wide).

Fill the slots to fit the photo assembly (Photo 6). Before you glue in the strips, assemble the frame around the assembly to test the fit. After gluing, flush each strip with the end. Then drill centered holes for the rare-earth magnets (Photo 7) and install them flush with the ends—make sure to orient the magnets' poles correctly! Secure the magnets with epoxy.

Snaps together and pulls apart, so changing photos is easy.

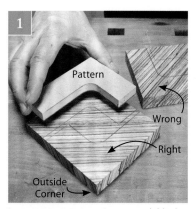

Lay out two corner sections on each blank. Make sure the grain runs across the outside corner. If it runs toward the corner, as on the blank in the background, the pieces will be impossible to rout.

Caution! The blade guard must be removed for this operation. Be careful!

Cut the short legs to final length using the miter gauge with a fence and a stop.

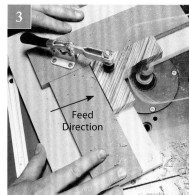

Rout the inside edges with a 1-in.-dia. pattern bit. Because of the grain's direction, you can only rout one leg at a time. Stop before the bit touches the adjacent leg or disastrous tearout will occur.

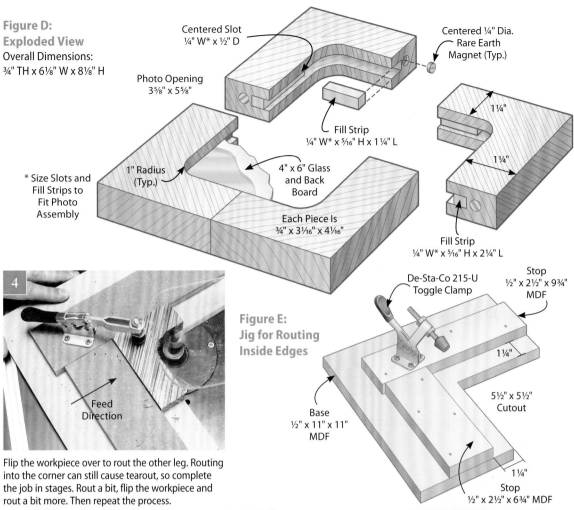

Figure D:
Exploded View
Overall Dimensions:
¾" TH x 6⅛" W x 8⅛" H

Centered Slot
¼" W* x ½" D

Centered ¼" Dia.
Rare Earth
Magnet (Typ.)

Photo Opening
3⅝" x 5⅝"

Fill Strip
¼" W* x ⁵⁄₁₆" H x 1¼" L

1" Radius
(Typ.)

4" x 6" Glass
and Back
Board

* Size Slots and
Fill Strips to
Fit Photo
Assembly

Each Piece Is
¾" x 3¹⁄₁₆" x 4¹⁄₁₆"

1¼"

1¼"

Fill Strip
¼" W* x ⁵⁄₁₆" H x 2¼" L

Figure E:
Jig for Routing
Inside Edges

De-Sta-Co 215-U
Toggle Clamp

Stop
½" x 2½" x 9¾"
MDF

1¼"

Base
½" x 11" x 11"
MDF

5½" x 5½"
Cutout

1¼"

Stop
½" x 2½" x 6¾" MDF

Flip the workpiece over to rout the other leg. Routing into the corner can still cause tearout, so complete the job in stages. Rout a bit, flip the workpiece and rout a bit more. Then repeat the process.

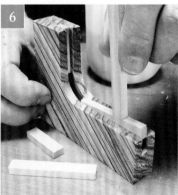

Rout a centered slot in each piece. Center the bit by eye. Then make two passes, one on each face. Rout halfway, as before, then flip the workpiece. Once the slot is established, you can rout against the grain to widen it.

Reduce the slots' depth to ³⁄₁₆-in. by gluing in fill strips. Leave the inside corner ½-in. deep, to accommodate the square corners of the glass.

Drill holes for the rare earth magnets using a fence and a stop block. The fence centers the hole between the faces; the stop block centers it between the edges.

Grooved Frame

This frame looks as if it's made from a single board (Fig. F). But it isn't. A board this wide could cup or twist, and seasonal movement could bind the glass and cause trouble. To minimize these potential problems, this frame is made by ripping plainsawn stock into thin pieces, standing them on edge and gluing them back together. This method creates a blank that's more stable than a solid board, because it has quartersawn grain, narrow pieces and multiple glue joints.

Start by crosscutting a 6-in.-wide by 30-in.-long board into three 10-in.-long sections. Then rip each section into 1 1/16-in.-wide pieces (Photo 1). This frame requires fifteen pieces. Glue the pieces together to form a 1 1/16-in.-thick blank

(Photo 2). Level the blank's top and bottom faces by sanding. Create the frame by cutting the blank apart and reassembling it (Photo 3). Rip the blank into three pieces, two that are 2 1/8-in. wide and one that's 5 5/8-in. wide, the height of the photo opening. Next, crosscut the wide center piece into three sections. The center section must be 3 1/2-in.-wide, the width of the photo opening. Glue the frame blank together (Photo 4). Knock out the center section. Then crosscut the ends of the blank to create 2-in.-wide frame rails. Joint or rip the two stiles to final width—make sure these widths are identical, so the photo opening is perfectly centered.

Follows the straight and narrow rout(e).

Figure F:
Exploded View
Overall dimensions:
1" TH x 7 1/2" W x 9 5/8" H

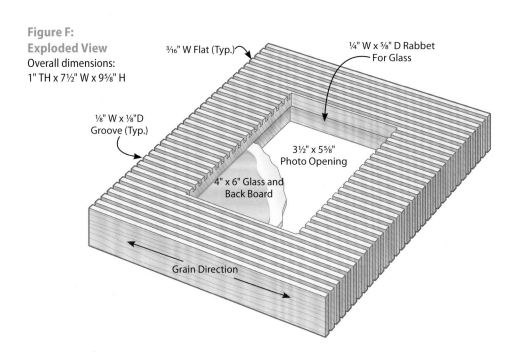

3/16" W Flat (Typ.)

1/4" W x 5/8" D Rabbet
For Glass

1/8" W x 1/8"D
Groove (Typ.)

3 1/2" x 5 5/8"
Photo Opening

4" x 6" Glass and
Back Board

Grain Direction

Rip 1¹⁄₁₆-in.-wide pieces from ¾-in.-thick blanks that have been cut to length. A thin-rip jig (Fig. G) makes the process simple and safe.

To glue the blank together, stand the pieces on end and clamp them between cauls. Cauls keep the pieces flush, to minimize sanding.

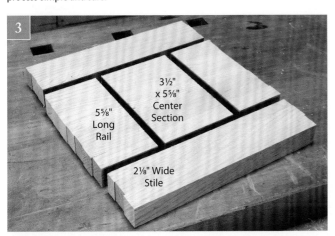

Rip the blank into three pieces. Then crosscut the center piece into three pieces. The outer pieces are the frame's stiles and rails. The middle section is exactly the size of the photo opening.

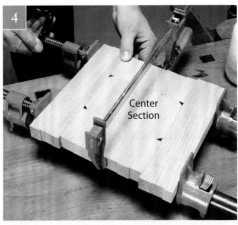

Glue the outer pieces back together to create the frame blank. The center section automatically creates the photo opening. Bevel its corners so it doesn't get stuck by glue squeeze-out.

Figure G: Jig for Ripping Thin Strips

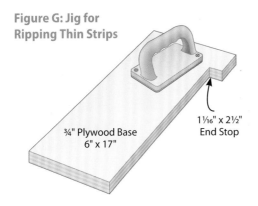

¾" Plywood Base
6" x 17"

1¹⁄₁₆" x 2½"
End Stop

Figure H: Sled for Routing Edges

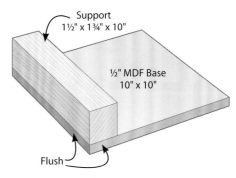

Support
1½" x 1¾" x 10"

½" MDF Base
10" x 10"

Flush

Set up for routing the grooves after installing a ⅛-in.-dia. spiral bit (Photo 5). Install sixteen ⁵/₁₆-in.-thick spacers at both ends of the fence. Firmly press stop blocks against the spacers and clamp them to the table. Rout the first groove on the face and both edges (Photos 6 and 7). Adjust the fence (Photo 8). From here on in, you rout two grooves on the face and edges between each fence adjustment (Photo 9).

Use a rabbeting bit with a ⅞-in.-dia. bearing to rout ¼-in.-wide glass rabbets. Square the corners with a chisel. The rabbeted opening should measure 6⅛-in. across the grain, to allow for seasonal movement around the 6-in.-tall glass and back board.

Position the fence so the frame's first groove will be exactly centered. Install spacers at both ends and clamp on stop blocks.

Rout the first groove on the face.

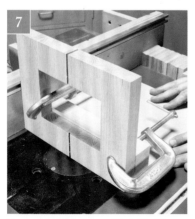

Use a sled with a support block (Fig. H) to rout the edges.

Remove one spacer from each side. The spacers' thickness determines the distance between the grooves. Reposition the fence against the remaining spacers and lock it in place.

Rout the remaining grooves in pairs. Rout one groove, then flip the frame end for end to rout the other groove. Ditto for routing the edges.

Picture Frames from Scrap

by RYAN VOGT

I finally found a great use for all those pieces of scrap wood that pile up around my shop: I make simple picture frames out of them. As you can see there's not much to them. The size shown here is for a 6- x 6-in.-square picture that I printed off my computer, but you can make them any size you want. I rout the groove on my router table using a ¼-in. straight bit. I add an extra layer of thin cardboard behind the picture and between the acrylic so these pieces fit snugly into the grooves. The parts are simply held together by friction but you can add some hot-melt glue if you want to make it more permanent.

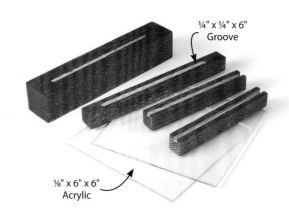

¼" x ¼" x 6"
Groove

⅛" x 6" x 6"
Acrylic

¾" x ¾" x 8"

¾" x ¾" x 5½"

1½" x 1½" x 8"

by JOCK *and* SUSAN HOLMEN

Craftsman Frame

PEGGED HALF-LAP JOINTS ARE THE CABINETMAKER'S WAY TO BUILD A BEAUTIFUL FRAME

P icture frames are pretty easy to make, except when it comes to putting the pieces together. Getting four mitered corners perfectly cut and glued can drive you batty! This frame uses a simpler approach—the half-lap, a traditional furniture maker's joint. It's very easy to make on the tablesaw and resembles a much more complicated mortise-and-tenon joint.

If you've never made a picture frame or lap joint before, this is a great project to start with. And it's easy to make a whole bunch of these frames at the same time. We'll show you an optional goof-proof sled that helps make cutting dozens of joints simple, safe and accurate.

Our frame is teak, a wood whose rich golden color beautifully complements most photos or artwork. Using quartersawn white oak would also look striking. This is a traditional Arts and Crafts-style frame, and quartered oak

Figure A: Exploded View

	Cutting List		
Overall dimensions: ¾" x 13⁵⁄₁₆" x 16¹⁄₁₆"			
Part	**Name**	**Qty.**	**Dimensions**
A	Stile	2	⅝" x 1⅛" x 16¹⁄₁₆"
B	Rail	2	¾" x 1¼" x 13⁵⁄₁₆"
C	Peg	4	¼" dia. x ¾" long

was the preferred wood of that era. If you've got some ¾ (2-in.) wood, you can make top-grade quartersawn pieces for this frame by ripping the board at an angle (see "Make Your Own Quartersawn Lumber," page 91).

We've sized the frame to fit precut matte and glass available at many craft stores, so you don't have to cut your own. The matte is 11 x 14 in. and fits an 8 x 10-in. photo.

You'll need a stacking dado set for your tablesaw to make the lap joints. (A wobble-type dado set won't work because it doesn't cut a flat bottom.) You'll also need a rabbeting bit for your router table (Photo 8). We recommend using a brad-point drill bit for the pegs that go into the frame's corners. This bit makes a cleaner entry hole than a standard twist bit.

The uprights, or stiles (A, Fig. A), of this frame are ⅝ in. thick. The cross pieces, or rails (B), are ¾ in. thick. If you don't have a planer to thin down pieces to ⅝ in., that's not a problem. The pieces are so narrow that you can make them the right thickness on your tablesaw. Just stand some ¾-in. pieces on edge and rip them to ⅝ in.

Begin by cutting the stiles and rails to final width and length (see Cutting List). At the same time, make two extra stiles and two extra rails from an inexpensive wood to use as test pieces when you cut the joints.

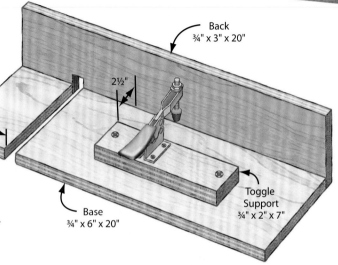

Back
¾" x 3" x 20"

2½"

Toggle
Support
¾" x 2" x 7"

Base
¾" x 6" x 20"

6"

**Figure B:
Dado Sled**

PROJECT REQUIREMENTS AT A GLANCE

Materials:
- 2 bd. ft. of hardwood lumber,
- One ¼-in. walnut dowel rod.

Tools:
- Tablesaw
- Planer
- Jointer
- Router table
- Drill press
- Flush-cut saw
- Chisel
- Mallet
- ¼-in. Drill bit
- ¼-in. Rabbeting router bit
- Planer
- Router
- ½-In. Flush-trim bit

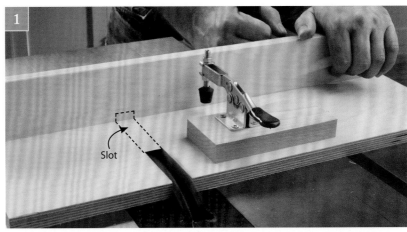

Build a sled to cut the half-lap joints (Fig. B). You could simply use a fence on your miter gauge, but this sled is more accurate, is safer and always delivers consistent results. Install a ¾-in. dado set in your saw and raise the blade ⅛ in. above the sled. Cut a slot through the sled's base and you're ready to go.

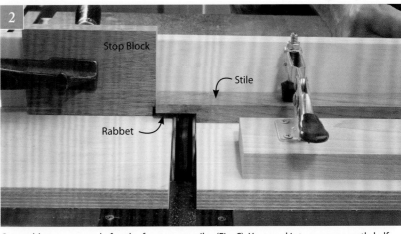

Cut a rabbet on one end of each of your spare stiles (Fig. C). Your goal is to remove exactly half the thickness. Clamp the stop block so the length of the rabbet matches the width of a rail. Two passes are necessary to cut the full rabbet.

Test the fit until the two test pieces are flush. The back of the frame will then be perfectly flat, which is important for accurately cutting the rabbet that holds the matte and glass. If the pieces aren't flush, adjust the height of the blade and try again. It's better to start with the blade too low rather than too high, because you can recut the same pieces. When you're satisfied, make these cuts on the ends of all the real stiles.

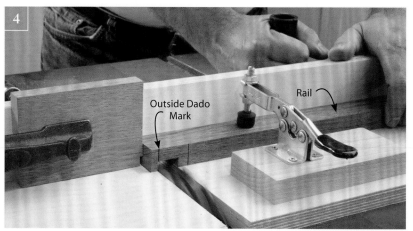

Cut the first half of the dadoes in all the rails with the blade at the same height as in Step 2. The full dado requires two overlapping cuts. You'll clamp the stop block in a different position for each cut. For the first cut, mark the dado on a test rail. Line up the outside mark with the right-hand cut in the sled.

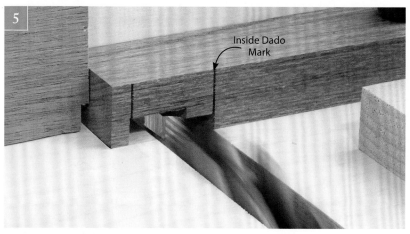

Cut the second half of the dado only in a test piece. Move the stop block so the inside dado mark lines up with the left-hand cut in the sled.

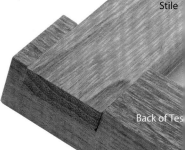

Test fit one corner. Your goal is to have the two pieces slip by each other to make a tight fit without requiring any force. If the joint is too tight, move the stop block and recut the test piece. If the joint is too loose, make the dado narrower by adding a piece or two of tape to the stop block's end. Try the new setting out on the second test piece. When you're satisfied with the fit, continue cutting the actual rails. Sand all the pieces to 150 grit. Slightly round all the edges with sandpaper.

Figure C: Half-Lap Joint

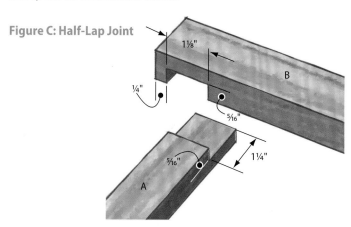

Caution! Hold the frame down with push pads to keep your hands out of harm's way.

Glue the frame together. You don't need much glue or clamping pressure. Spring clamps work fine, so you don't have to worry about marring freshly sanded surfaces. Remove any squeezed-out glue with a sharp stick before the glue hardens. Wipe off the stick's glue on a damp rag as you go.

Rout a rabbet all the way around the frame's back (Figure D). Use a rabbeting bit with a ball-bearing pilot. The pilot rides on the inside of the frame to control the depth of cut. Make this cut in two passes. Raise the router bit so the first cut is ¼ in. high; then raise the bit so the second cut is ⅜ in. high.

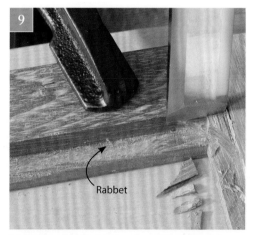

Figure D: Rabbet
Overall rabbet opening: 11¹⁄₁₆" x 14¹⁄₁₆"

Square the rabbet's corners using a wide chisel. Cut across the grain first, then with the grain, then across again, and so on, taking small cuts to avoid splintering the wood. When the rabbet is complete, order the glass. It should be ¹⁄₁₆ in. smaller than the opening. To be on the safe side, your best bet is to give the frame to the glass cutter. (Precut 11 x 14-in. glass to fit the frame is also widely available.)

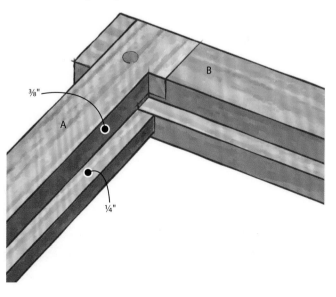

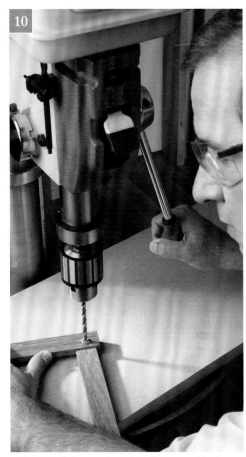

Cut off the dowels with a flush-cut saw. Hold the blade down against the frame, press into the dowel and saw slowly. A good flush-cut saw shouldn't leave any saw marks on your frame, but it's a good idea to practice first on the back of the frame. Only a minimum of cleanup sanding is necessary. Finish the frame with shellac or varnish.

Drill a hole all the way through each corner of the frame using a brad-point bit. Glue ¼-in. dowels into each hole. Use a contrasting wood to emphasize this accent. Small dowels vary in diameter, so it's a good idea to drill a test hole first. You may need to switch to a slightly undersize bit to get a good fit. The brad point bit I used comes in ¹⁄₆₄-in. sizes.

Fit the glass, matte, photo or art into the frame and secure with fasteners. For more information on installing these materials, see "How To Mount Artwork," page 20. Attach hangers or eye hooks and wire onto the back of the frame.

MAKE YOUR OWN QUARTERSAWN LUMBER

If you've got some spare 8/4 (2-in.) lumber lying around your shop, it's easy to transform it into stunning quartersawn wood for your picture frame. Quartersawn figure in almost every wood is really something special, and quite different from species to species. Even an ordinary piece of thick oak, maple or cherry has a surprise waiting within it.

Cherry

Maple

Oak

Mark both ends of a milled 8/4 board with a series of parallel lines that run at right angles to the growth rings. Tilt the blade to match the angle of the first cut—just eyeball it. Move the fence and make the second cut at the same angle.

Next, turn the board around and repeat the same procedure for the other outside edge. Continue to work your way from the outside in, so the last cuts you make are for the center pieces, where your drawn lines are almost vertical.

Return the blade to 90 degrees and saw off the angled edges. Make sure the edge that runs along the fence has the point facing up. If it faces down, it could get trapped underneath the fence. Run the pieces through the planer, and you're ready to make a very special picture frame.

by TIM JOHNSON

Fab Frames

NO MITERS AND NO FUSS! MULTIPLES AND COOL VARIATIONS ARE EASY

Forget about cutting and fitting miter joints the next time you make a picture frame. Scrap wood, a saber saw, a fence-equipped router table and three common router bits are all you need to make this one.

The process couldn't be simpler: Saw and rout an opening for a 4- x 6-in. image in the center of a board; then rout flutes around the face (Fig. A). This procedure is ideal for making multiple frames, and changing the pattern is so easy that you can rout several different-looking frames at the same time (see "Amazing Variations," page 94).

Those large offcuts you've been saving are perfect for this project, but you can also make frame blanks by gluing up narrow stock. Hardwoods such as birch, maple, cherry, beech, walnut and poplar are good choices.

Shape the Blank

1. Glue together a template sized precisely, as shown in Fig. B. Drill shank holes for the screws that will hold this template to the frame blank.

2. Plane wood for the blank to ½-in. thickness. This piece must be at least 12 in. long to safely pass through your planer. You can skip this step and use thicker stock, of course—your finished frame will just look heftier.

3. Cut the frame blank to size, ⅛ in. wider and longer than your template.

4. Center the template on the blank and attach it with one screw. With a pencil, trace the picture opening onto the blank. Mark the template so you'll use the same screw hole when you remount it in Step 6.

5. After you've removed the template, drill access holes for the saber-saw blade in the blank, near the corners of the picture opening. Then rough-saw the opening ⅛ in. or less away from the traced line.

Five Easy Steps

1.   2.   3.   4.   5.

Step 1: Rout a rectangular picture opening in the center of a piece of wood. Steps 2–4: Rout flutes around the face. Step 5: trim the edges.

Amazing Variations

The setup used to create the basic fab frame, shown above, lends itself to a surprising number of interesting variations. For example, rout a single middle flute on each side. Or rout outside and inside flutes only (see the double dip frame, right). You can rout only vertical flutes on the stiles, or only horizontal flutes on the rails.

Creating the diamond, sunburst and waterfall frames requires routing additional rows of flutes. Simply install as many ½-in.-wide spacers as you need before routing the first flute.

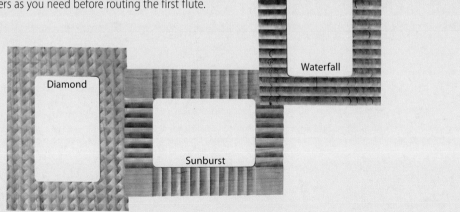

Double Dip

Waterfall

Diamond

Sunburst

Figure A: Exploded View

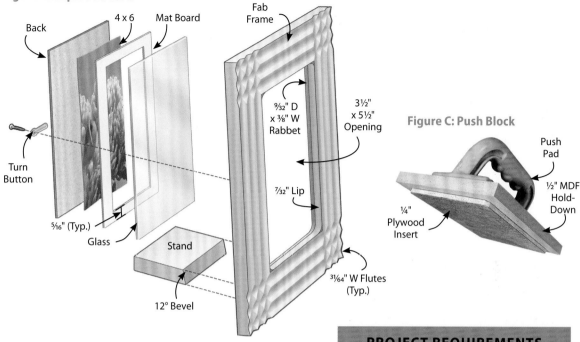

Back

4 x 6

Mat Board

Fab Frame

Turn Button

⁹⁄₃₂" D x ³⁄₈" W Rabbet

3½" x 5½" Opening

⁷⁄₃₂" Lip

⁵⁄₁₆" (Typ.)

Glass

Stand

12° Bevel

³¹⁄₆₄" W Flutes (Typ.)

Figure C: Push Block

Push Pad

½" MDF Hold-Down

¼" Plywood Insert

Figure B: Routing Template

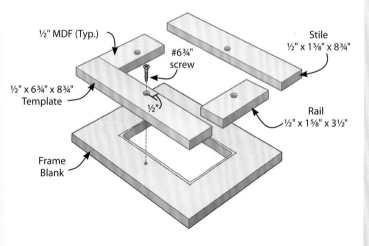

½" MDF (Typ.)

#6 ¾" screw

½" x 6¾" x 8¾" Template

½"

Stile ½" x 1⅝" x 8¾"

Rail ½" x 1⅝" x 3½"

Frame Blank

PROJECT REQUIREMENTS AT A GLANCE

Materials:
- 1 sq. ft. of ½-in. MDF
- One frame blank and stand
- One sheet of glass
- One piece of mat board
- One piece of ⅛-in. hardboard

Hardware:
- One ¾ No. 6 screw
- Four turn buttons
- One EaselMate frame stand (optional)

Tools:
- Planer
- Tablesaw
- Drill press or hand drill
- ½-in. drill bit
- Saber saw
- Router table with router and fence
- Flush-trim bit
- Rabbeting bit
- ¾-in.-dia. round-nose bit (also called a core-box bit)
- Chisel
- Two 8-in.-capacity clamps

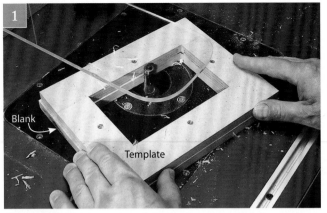

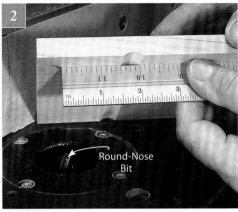

This picture frame is just a piece of wood with a rectangular hole cut in it. After rough-cutting the picture opening in an oversize frame blank, use the routing template (Fig. B, above) and a flush-trim bit to cleanly rout both the inside and outside edges.

Dial in the flute's width by adjusting the bit's height. Make test cuts in a scrap piece until the flute measures slightly less than ½ in. wide. It's easy to eyeball this measurement on a coarse scale: Just sight along both graduations' inside edges.

6. Remount the template using all four screws.

7. Using a flush-trim bit, rout the blank to match the template (Photo 1). Feed the blank clockwise to rout the inside and counterclockwise to rout the outside. Tear-out may occur at the corners when you rout the blank's outside edges, but it's OK, because the routed blank is still oversize. It will be trimmed to its final size later.

8. Complete the picture opening by installing a rabbeting bit and routing a 9/32-in.-deep x 3/8-in.-wide rabbet for the glass, mat board, image and back. Square the rabbet's corners with a chisel.

Rout the Flutes

I'll explain how to rout the basic frame, but you can use the same steps to create several variations.

The frame's ½-in.-wide flutes are routed with a ¾-in.-dia. round-nose bit that's partially recessed in the router table. This setup creates shallow flutes that look much better than the deep flutes a ½-in.-dia. bit would create.

9. Raise the bit to set the flute's width (Photo 2). The flutes should measure about 1/64 in. less than ½-in. wide. Flutes wider than ½ in. won't work.

10. Lock the fence in position to rout the outside flutes (Photo 3). When properly located, these flutes leave 1 in. for the two remaining flutes.

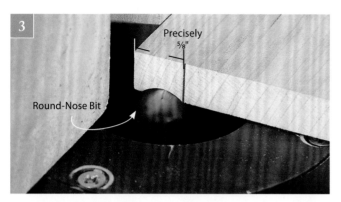

Set the router table's fence to rout the outside flutes. Draw a line on your test piece exactly ⅝ in. from the edge. Then make test cuts until the flute's inner edge precisely aligns with the line.

Install a pair of ½-in.-wide spacers and a stop behind the fence. This setup makes it easy to accurately reposition the fence for routing the middle and inside flutes.

Rout the flutes, starting at the outside edge. To rout the middle flutes, simply remove one spacer and reposition the fence. Remove both spacers to rout the inside flutes.

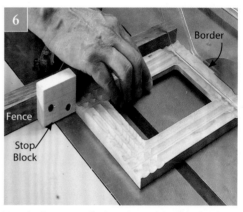

Trim the frame to its final size by sawing off the borders. Trimming the frame after routing the flutes eliminates the possibility of router tear-out on the outside edges.

11. Mill a pair of long spacers exactly ½ in. wide and install them behind the router table's fence. A clamped-on stop holds them in place (Photo 4).

12. Rout the outside flutes all around the frame blank (Photo 5). A shop-made push block with an insert that fits into the rabbeted picture opening makes routing super-easy and safe (Fig. C).

13. Loosen the fence and remove one spacer. Firmly push the fence against the remaining spacer and clamp it in place. This adjustment moves the fence exactly ½ in. so you can rout the middle flutes. As you rout across the grain, use a slow feed rate to minimize tear-out between the two flutes.

14. To rout the inner flutes, simply remove the remaining spacer and reposition the fence against the stop.

Finishing Touches

15. Trim the frame's sides on the tablesaw (Photo 6).

16. Sand the flutes to eliminate ridges and blend uneven spacing. Sanding also gets rid of tear-out between the flutes. I use Tadpole contour sanders to help with this job, but a detail sander or sandpaper wrapped around a dowel will also do the trick.

17. To make a stand for the frame, saw a 12-degree bevel on one edge of a long blank. Then cut the stand to size.

18. Glue the stand to the back of the frame. You don't have to use clamps. Just brush a coat of glue on the stand's beveled edge. With the frame lying on its face, press the stand onto the frame, flush with the bottom edge. Rub the stand back and forth to set the glue; then let the assembly dry. As an alternative, the EaselMate frame stand doesn't require gluing and it's removable (see page 75).

19. Apply your favorite finish to both sides of the frame. I prefer aerosol-spray finishes for small jobs like this, because they're fast, but you won't have to worry about drips if you choose a wipe-on finish. Or you could be adventurous (see "Great Fun To Finish," right).

20. Install the glass, mat board, image and the back. Then screw on the turn buttons. You should be able to use the screw holes that remain from fastening the template.

Great Fun To Finish

My children had a blast painting and staining these frames. They quickly discovered how easy it was to highlight the flutes by sanding the finish or by adding additional colors.

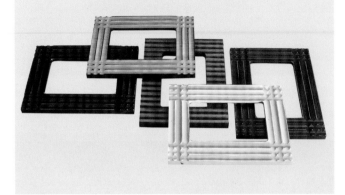

Cutting List

Overall Dimensions: ½" x 6½" x 8½"
Picture Opening: 3½" x 5½"

Part	Qty.	Dimensions
Frame blank	1	½" x 6⅞" x 8⅞"
Stand	1	½" x 2" x 2½"*
Glass	1	³⁄₃₂" x 4³⁄₁₆" x 6³⁄₁₆"
Matte board	1	¹⁄₁₆" x 4¼" x 6¼"
Back	1	⅛"** x 4¼" x 6¼"
Frame template	1	½" x 6¾" x 8¾"
Template stile	2	½" x 1⅝" x 8¾"
Template rail	2	½" x 1⅝" x 3½"
Push-block hold-down	1	½" x 5¼" x 7¼"
Push-block insert	1	¼"*** x 4¼" x 6¼"

* one edge beveled 12 degrees ** hardboard *** plywood

CLOSE AN OPEN MITER

by BYRON SCOTT

I didn't notice this misfit miter until glue-up. Fortunately, there's an easy way to hide narrow gaps like this one. Before the glue dries, rub the corner with a hard, rounded object, like a big drill bit. Rubbing crushes the wood fibers inward and closes the gap. The fibers stiffen as the glue dries. This leaves a rounded corner that's barely noticeable unless the gap is really wide.

SPRING CLAMP FOR MITERS

by BERT HERRICK

Spring clamps are easily converted to miter clamps by adding swivel jaws. Remove the vinyl tips, then hacksaw a ½" long slot down the center of the metal jaws. Use needle-nose vise-grips to fold down the two halves of each jaw, and then drill a hole for a small bolt or rivet. To make the swivel jaws, snap off two pieces, ¾"–1" long, from an old hacksaw blade. Drill holes through their centers and fasten them between your spring clamp's folded tips. For extra holding power, double the blades at each tip. Make sure the teeth point towards the clamp's mouth for maximum gripping power.

by LINDSEY DILL *and* TOM BOCKMAN

Lindsey Dill's Fabulous Frames

AN INGENIOUS YOUNG WOODWORKER DISCOVERS THE FUN OF JIG-MAKING

Last fall, Mr. Bockman, my shop teacher, presented plans for several woodworking projects to my class and asked us each to choose one to build. The frames were covered with routed flutes that looked awesome. The story said making variations was easy and that you could make lots of frames at the same time. Plus, they didn't have to be mitered. That sounded great!

Mr. Bockman's Challenge

Following the step-by-step directions in the story made the project take too long for our one-hour shop classes. So Mr. Bockman asked if I could come up with changes that would simplify the project and save time.

My Response

I knew right away the first change I would make. The original directions called for using a form to rout the frame blanks, so they'd all be the same size. The form was made out of several pieces that had to be glued together, which I thought was silly. I made my form by cutting a single piece to size and then routing out the center. My form measures 9-in. by 11-in. and its center opening is 4½-in. by 6½-in., perfect for 5x7 photos. After I've routed each frame and removed it from the form, I rout a rabbet around the inside opening, for the photo.

I thought of my second change after following the directions to rout the flutes in a frame blank. The directions called for using the router table and a fence to do this job. The fence had to be precisely set up to rout the first flutes and then had to be adjusted several times to rout the remaining flutes. Bor-ing! And after completing a few frames, I was frustrated, because I could only rout flutes in straight lines.

My First Jig

After discovering that I could make wavy flutes with a template and a hand-held router, I designed a jig with rows of evenly spaced holes to index the template (see "My First Jig," page 102). Cutouts securely hold the frame blank vertically and horizontally. I use straight bits or core-box bits to create the flutes.

My Second Jig

What if I could move the frame as easily as I could now move the template? Then I could rout flutes diagonally across the frames. I tried drilling the jig's indexing holes in a circle around the cutouts, but I couldn't get the spacing right. So instead of spinning the template, I decided to spin the frame. By this time I was tired of drilling holes, so I figured out how to get rid of them, too. My second jig has a rotating circular insert and a T-square fence (see "My Second Jig," page 103). This time the routing templates attach to the fence and the fence clamps to the jig.

Lindsey Dill shows some of the frames that she made in her woodworking class at Prescott High School in Prescott, Arizona.

My First Jig

My first jig allows routing flutes horizontally and vertically. I can rout straight, curved, V-shaped or wavy flutes, depending on the shape of the template. I like making the rows slightly asymmetrical, so I follow the template with the corner of a square-based laminate trimmer.

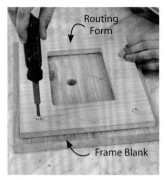

Routing Form

Frame Blank

To fit in my jigs, the frames all have to be the same size. I attach oversize blanks to a precisely-sized form. After marking and rough-sawing the frame's center cutout, I rout each blank to match the form.

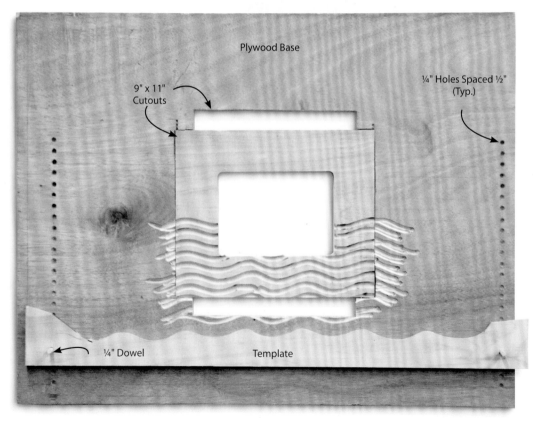

Plywood Base

9" x 11" Cutouts

¼" Holes Spaced ½" (Typ.)

¼" Dowel   Template

My Second Jig

My second jig is more versatile. The T-square fence clamps at any point, so I can vary the flutes' spacing. All of my templates fit, so the flutes follow any pattern, and the frame rotates, so I can rout flutes across it at any angle.

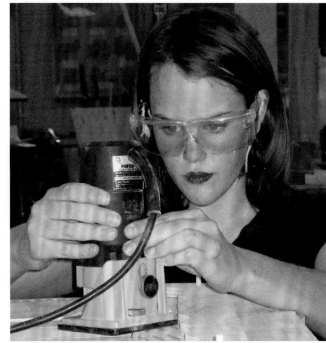

Lindsey's jigs make it easy to create frames with straight, curved or wavy patterns.

"Lindsey's problem-solving and imaginative solutions have made her fabulous frames a popular student project choice."

—Tom Bockman, Prescott High
   School woodworking instructor

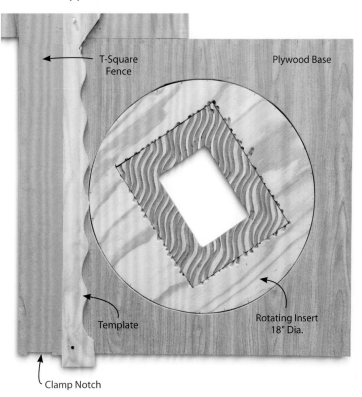

T-Square
Fence

Plywood Base

Template

Rotating Insert
18" Dia.

Clamp Notch

by LUKE HARTLE

Sycamore Hallway Mirror

WEEKEND PROJECT USES BEAUTIFUL WOOD, INVISIBLE HINGES, AND SIMPLE JOINERY

My front hallway is the most heavily traveled, and usually the most cluttered, space in my home. Keys are tossed here and there, notes are scattered and the mail keeps getting lost. Tired of misplacing small but important items, I found a decorative way to keep everything together and organized. No more misplaced bills and no more lost keys.

This hallway mirror presented me with the perfect opportunity to display some highly figured English sycamore I had recently acquired. The design is simple yet elegant, allowing the wood to shine. It is the first thing people see when they enter my home.

Materials and Construction

The frame is constructed with quick, easy biscuit joinery. Trim-head screws are used to attach the brackets, the lidded box and the cap piece on the frame. I chose these screws because their tiny heads are less visible and less prone to splitting thin parts, such as the brackets. Screws also allow the entire project to be disassembled for easier finishing.

Before making any cuts, lay out the pieces to maximize the wood yield. Build visual harmony into the project by laying out the box sides end to end so the grain flows around the box when it is assembled.

Hidden barrel hinges give the box a clean, seamless appearance and allow the lid to double as a shelf. Solid brass pegs add beauty to the mirror and are perfect for hanging keys. The large mirror stands ready for a last-second glance before I walk out the door.

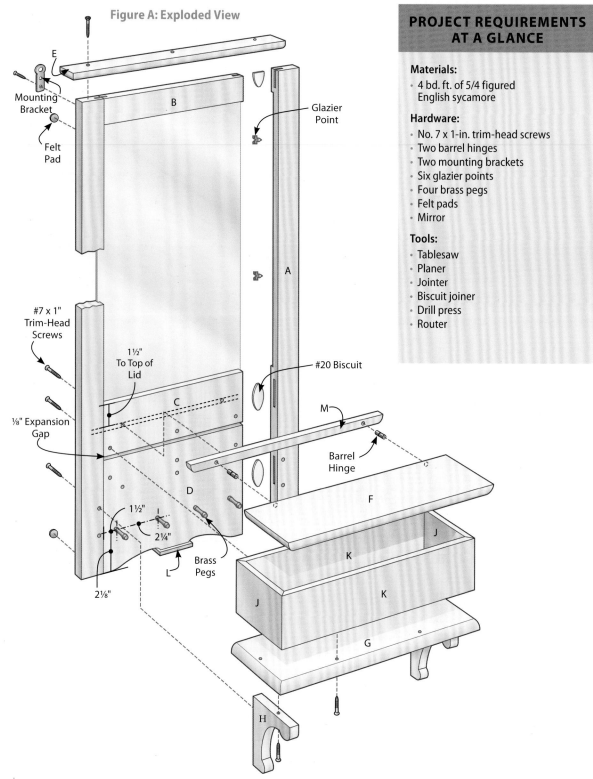

Figure A: Exploded View

E

Mounting
Bracket

Felt
Pad

B

Glazier
Point

#7 x 1"
Trim-Head
Screws

1½"
To Top of
Lid

⅛" Expansion
Gap

A

#20 Biscuit

C

M

Barrel
Hinge

D

F

1½"

2¼"

2⅛"

L

Brass
Pegs

J

K

K

J

G

H

PROJECT REQUIREMENTS AT A GLANCE

Materials:
- 4 bd. ft. of 5/4 figured English sycamore

Hardware:
- No. 7 x 1-in. trim-head screws
- Two barrel hinges
- Two mounting brackets
- Six glazier points
- Four brass pegs
- Felt pads
- Mirror

Tools:
- Tablesaw
- Planer
- Jointer
- Biscuit joiner
- Drill press
- Router

This project would also look great built with some straight-grained oak or pine, but I went all out and used figured English sycamore. My supplier requires a minimum purchase of $200 (roughly 7 bd. ft.). This is double the amount of lumber needed to build one project, so I simply decided to build two and give one as a gift. You can also combine your order for this project with other wood to reach the $200 threshold.

Build the Frame

1. Lay out the project parts on rough lumber (Photo 1). The wood gets resawn so you only need to lay out pieces for one mirror to make two. Planning before cutting allows you to match color and grain patterns and maximize the yield, which is especially important on precious wood. Lay out the brackets together on a piece of wood large enough to be planed and jointed before you cut them out.

2. Cut and mill all the parts. I opted to use ⁵⁄₄ stock because it minimizes waste and can be resawn into thinner pieces.

Join the frame parts using biscuits. On the narrow top rail, offset the slot so the biscuit protrudes out the top of the frame. It can be trimmed off later and completely covered by the top.

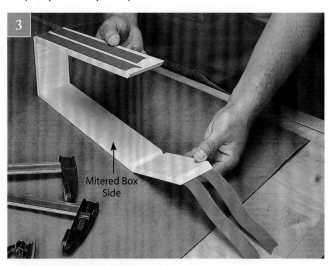

Position the box parts on two strips of masking tape. Spread glue and fold the pieces together. Use the overhanging tape to strap the last miter together. Square the box and snug the miters together with clamps.

**Figure C:
Bottom Rail Cutout**

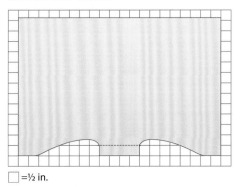

□ =½ in.

Figure B: Brackets

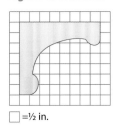

□ =½ in.

Use a photocopier to enlarge Figure B and Figure C images 400 percent and then 115 percent to make a ½-in. grid.

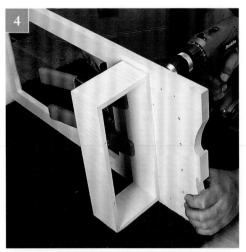

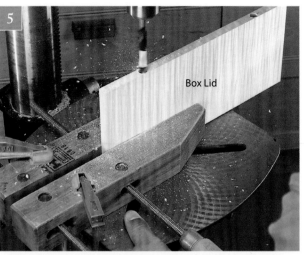

Screw the assembled box sides to the frame and build the rest of the box on the frame. Using this approach, it's easier to get the box lid and bottom to fit tightly against the mirror frame.

Drill holes in the box lid for the barrel hinges. Barrel hinges can be fussy to install. In this case, predrilling the hinge holes in the box lid and then ripping the hinge rail guarantees perfect alignment.

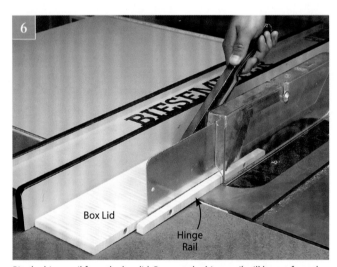

Rip the hinge rail from the box lid. Because the hinge rail will be cut from the box lid (see Step 13), the holes must be ⅛ in. deeper than the length of the hinge to account for the stock the tablesaw blade removed.

Place the hinges in the holes of the hinge rail. Tighten the screws just enough so the hinges can move in and out with pressure but do not slide freely.

Brass Pegs

3. Enlarge the pattern (Fig. C) to full size and trace it onto the bottom rail (D). Rough-cut the pattern on a bandsaw and then smooth the final shape on a sanding drum or a spindle sander. Trim off the waste piece.

4. Mark and drill the holes for the brass pegs on the bottom rail using a drill press (Fig. A).

5. Make the decorative cap (L). Ease the cap's edges and glue the cap to the bottom rail.

6. Join the frame pieces (Fig. A) using biscuits. Leave a ⅛-in. gap between the middle and bottom rails for cross-grain expansion. Offset the top rail slot so the biscuits hang out the top edge (Photo 2). Trim the biscuits flush after the glue has set.

7. Route a rabbet for the mirror around the back side of the frame. Square the corners using a chisel.

8. Attach the top (E) to the frame. Shape the front and side edges with a ¼-in. round-over bit, and screw the top in place (Fig. A).

Build the Box

9. Miter the box sides (J, K) on a sliding miter saw or with a miter gauge on the tablesaw.

10. Glue up the box (Photo 3). As long as the miters have been cut correctly, the box will fold up easily and the tape will hold the pieces together. Place the box in a framing square to nudge the box square and use a clamp to tighten the joints, if necessary.

11. Attach the box to the frame (Photo 4, Fig. A).

12. Drill holes for the hinges in the box lid (Photo 5). Secure the lid in a hand-screw clamp to make sure the holes are drilled straight, and clamp everything to the table so nothing moves.

13. Cut the hinge rail from the box lid (Photo 6) by ripping a strip, through the holes, ½ in. from the back edge of the box lid.

14. Screw the hinge rail to the frame and the box bottom to the box sides and frame (Fig. A).

15. Shape the brackets (H) from the pattern (Fig. B). Rough-cut the design on the bandsaw and sand each bracket smooth. Screw the brackets to the frame and to the box bottom (Fig. A).

Install the Barrel Hinges

16. Install the barrel hinges in the lid first and then place the hinges in the holes of the hinge rail (Photo 7).

17. Set the hinges using thin spacers, such as playing cards (Photo 8). Place the cards between the lid and the hinge rail and lightly push down on the lid. Gently open the lid and tighten the set screws. The lid should close tightly with only a slight gap between the lid and hinge rail.

8

Use playing cards to set the gap between the lid and hinge rail. The perfect fit has a nominal gap between the lid and hinge spacer, but allows the lid to close completely. If the lid does not close completely, double up the cards.

9

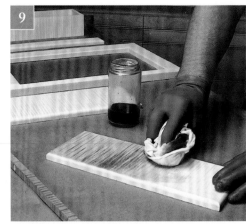

Disassemble the project's parts—except for the frame—to sand and finish. Every other piece can easily be sanded and finished individually, nearly eliminating the need to work in tight corners.

10

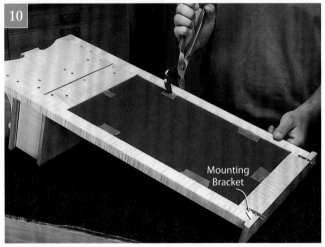

Mounting Bracket

Secure the mirror with glazier points. Place tape below each point and on the pliers' jaws to prevent scratches. Stick a few felt pads on the back of the frame to keep the frame from rubbing against the wall.

Add the Finishing Touches

18. Disassemble the project and finish (Photo 9). After everything is finished, reassemble the project.

19. Add the mounting brackets and pegs and install the mirror (Photo 10). Hang and enjoy.

Barrel Hinge

Cutting List
Overall Dimensions: 27¾" x 14" x 6"

Part	Name	Qty.	Material	Dimension
A	Frame stile	2	Sycamore	¾" x 1½" x 27¼"
B	Top frame rail	1	Sycamore	¾" x 1½" x 10"
C	Middle frame rail	1	Sycamore	¾" x 3" x 10"
D	Bottom frame rail	1	Sycamore	¾" x 6⅝" x 10"
E	Top	1	Sycamore	½" x 1¾" x 14"
F	Box lid	1	Sycamore	½" x 5⅜" x 12¾"
G	Box bottom	1	Sycamore	½" x 5¼" x 12¾"
H	Bracket	2	Sycamore	7⁄16" x 4" x 3½"
J	Short box side	2	Sycamore	⅜" x 2¾" x 4⅞"
K	Long box side	2	Sycamore	⅜" x 2¾" x 12"
L	Decorative cap	1	Sycamore	¼" x ⅞" x 2⅜"
M	Hinge rail *	1	Sycamore	½" x ½" x 12¾"

*Cut from box lid (F)

REINFORCE SHORT MITERS

by GARY WENTZ

To strengthen miter joints in narrow stock, use face frame biscuits. They're like standard biscuits but smaller (about 1³⁄₁₆ in. long), so you can use them in stock as narrow as 1 inch. To cut the slots, use a ⁵⁄₃₂-in.-thick slot cutter in your router table. Set the router fence so the bit cuts a ⁵⁄₁₆-in.-deep slot. Then clamp 45-degree guides to your router table. The guides make it easy to feed the workpiece into the slot cutter. Use one guide (A) for one end (A) and the other guide (B) for the other end (B). Test your setup before cutting actual parts of your project.

Slot Cutter

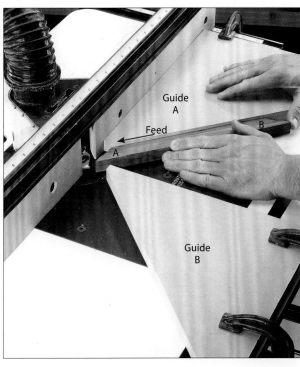

Guide A

Feed

B

A

Guide B

by RANDY JOHNSON

Oak Hallway Mirror

STEP-BY-STEP INSTRUCTIONS FOR CREATING AN HEIRLOOM

Made of quartersawn white oak, with lines and a finish that give it an Arts and Crafts look, this mirror could pass as an heirloom from grandma's attic. Just follow our step-by-step directions and you'll be hanging your new mirror by next weekend.

Build the Frame

1. Start by milling the rails and stiles to size. Cut the lap joints with a dado blade and an accurately set miter gauge (Photo 1).

2. With the lap joints cut, dry clamp the frame to make sure all the parts fit properly. Then glue and clamp the frame (Photo 2).

3. When dry, remove the clamps and sand flush any variation at the joints.

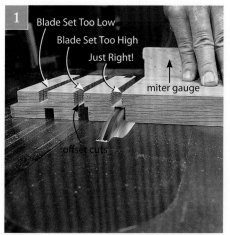

1 Blade Set Too Low
Blade Set Too High
Just Right!
miter gauge
offset cuts

Make test cuts to set the depth-of-cut for the lap joints. Make one pass on a piece of scrap that's the same thickness as your frame material. Then flip the test piece over and make another pass. Offset cuts allow you to determine the necessary adjustments even if the blade is set too high. Adjust the blade depth until the two cuts just meet.

2 ❶ Spring Clamps First
❷ Then Pipe Clamps
❸ Replace Spring Clamps With Hand Clamps

Clamp the glued-up frame. Start by holding the glued joints together with spring clamps. Add bar clamps to pull the joints tight. Replace the spring clamps with hand or C-clamps. Be careful not to overtighten the bar clamps or the frame may bow.

Figure A: Hall Mirror Exploded View

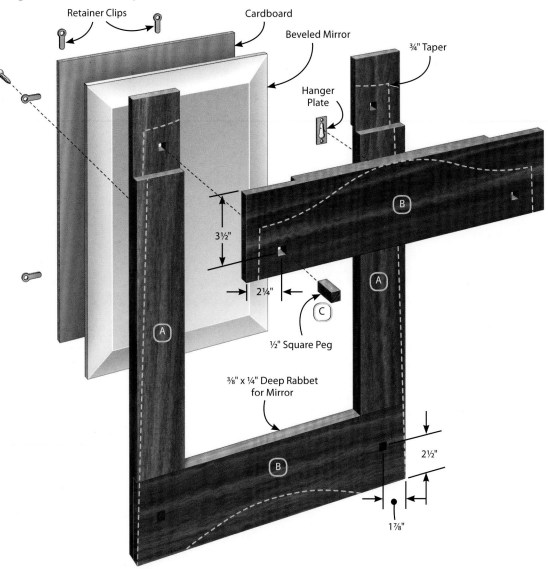

Retainer Clips

Cardboard

Beveled Mirror

¾" Taper

Hanger Plate

3½"

2¼"

C

½" Square Peg

⅜" x ¼" Deep Rabbet for Mirror

A

B

A

B

2½"

1⅞"

Figure B: Top and Bottom Profile Grid

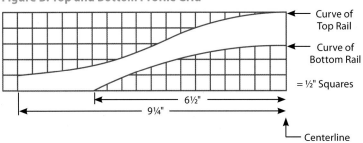

Curve of Top Rail

Curve of Bottom Rail

= ½" Squares

6½"

9¼"

Centerline

Cutting List			
Overall Dimensions 28" H x 20" W x 1" D			
Part	**Qty**	**Dimensions**	**Name**
A	2	1" x 3½" x 28"	Side Stiles
B	2	1" x 5" x 20"	Top & Bottom Rails
C	4	½" x ½" x 1⅛"	Pegs*

*includes extra length for sanding off

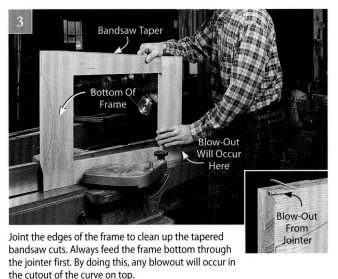

Joint the edges of the frame to clean up the tapered bandsaw cuts. Always feed the frame bottom through the jointer first. By doing this, any blowout will occur in the cutout of the curve on top.

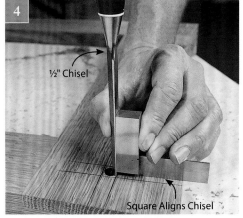

Finish chopping the through mortise with a ½-in. bench chisel. Use a square to help align your chisel for a straight cut.

4. Next, lay out the side tapers, the curves and the locations for the pegs (Figs. A and B). Cut the side tapers on the bandsaw and clean up the tapers on the jointer (Photo 3).

5. Bandsaw the top and bottom curves and sand smooth.

6. Chuck a ½-in. bit into your drill press and drill out the centers for the four pegs.

7. Finish chopping the through mortises with a ½-in. chisel (Photo 4).

8. With the mortises cut, mill the pegs 1⅛-in. long. Pound them in place with a little glue and sand off flush.

9. Using a ⅜-in. rabbeting bit with a bearing, cut the rabbet for the mirror.

10. Chisel the corners square and take measurements for the mirror. Allow for a 1/16-in. gap all around. Most hardware stores that sell glass and mirrors can custom order a beveled mirror to your dimensions.

Tip If you have a ½-in. hollow-chisel bit, you can use it to cut the peg mortises. Drill out a block of wood to protect the end of the chisel. The hollow chisel is a handy tool for squaring the rabbet in the back of the mirror, too.

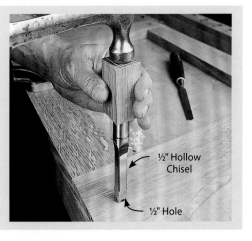

Apply Old Growth Solutions' two-part Fumed Oak stain with a synthetic brush. The activator solution goes on first. After it dries, apply the catalyst solution. Use a clean brush for each solution. Be sure to wear gloves or your hands will end up looking like "fumed oak."

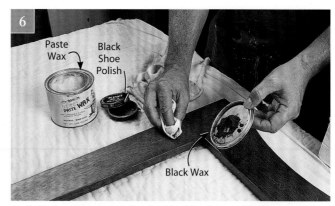

Apply black wax for a quick, hand-rubbed finish. To make black wax, mix one part black shoe polish with three parts paste wax. Apply three or four coats of this mixture onto the stained wood. Let the wax dry between applications and buff out each coat before applying the next.

The Finish

For that "seasoned" look, we used Old Growth Solutions' Fumed Oak stain. It's an easy-to-use, two-part product that goes on like water with no strong smell (Photo 5). This product does raise the grain, so we suggest pre-raising the grain with a moist rag. Let the wood dry and lightly sand off the high spots. It's best to wear gloves for the final sanding because fingerprints left on the surface of the wood can react with the solution, producing a blotchy look.

Let the stain dry overnight. Old Growth Solutions' stain is compatible with any finish, but for a quick, hand rubbed look we used black wax as the final finish (Photo 6). Black wax colors the pores and gives the frame a mellow antique look.

The Hang Up

Back the mirror with a couple of layers of matte board or a layer of corrugated cardboard and secure with eight panel retainer clips. Then, add a wall hanger to the back of the top rail. These items are available from various sources. Now find a prominent wall on which to hang your mirror. Step back and see who's the finest woodworker of them all!

Oops!

Our mirror was a bit undersized, so we used a neat trick that keeps the mirror centered in the opening. Cut some triangular wedges out of a soft wood like pine or basswood. Center the mirror in the rabbet and add a touch of glue to the back of the wedge. Rub the wedge against the edge of the rabbet with a slight back and forth motion to set the glue joint while applying enough downward pressure to wedge the mirror in place. Plane the blocks flush with the frame. The soft blocks support the mirror, but will compress if the frame expands.

TAPE SIMPLIFIES GLUING MITER JOINTS

by MARTHA JONES

Let's face it: Gluing mitered frames is a hassle. You need four, five or even six hands—or the time-honored shop staple, masking tape. I like the good, strong blue kind. You'll need one piece for each corner. Lay the masking tape face up and place the joint's pieces tip to tip on the tape. Spread a thin, even coat of glue on both faces of the joint. Fold together the pieces for each joint using the tape as a hinge. For small frames, the tape alone can be enough to hold the joint while the glue dries. On large frames, the tape securely holds the parts in place while you apply clamps.

Index

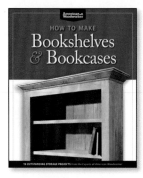

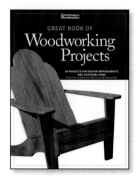
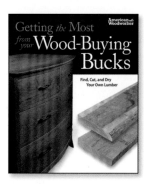
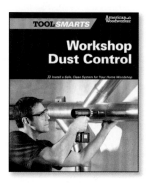
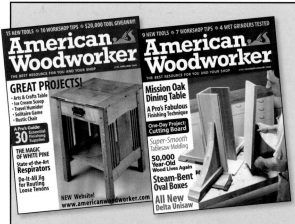